FOREWORD

In the current contentious political atmosphere in which friends, if they wish to stay friends, strictly avoid the slightest political discussion, many might wistfully wonder how things might have been different if certain events had not occurred and if certain personages who became President would not have done so.

If, in one alternative universe the Gary Hart campaign of 1988 had not been derailed and Hart would have gone on to become President, how might things have been different? If Hart had served two terms, would he have faced a primary challenge from Bill Clinton in 1996 that would have put Clinton on the fast track much as Hart had been put on the fast track following his challenge of Mondale in 1984, or would that have been the end of Clinton's career?

Would George H.W. Bush have succeeded him in 1996? Would Bush again have been a one term President and opened the door for the likes of a Democrat such as Clinton in 2000? How would Clinton have handled 9/11? If Clinton served two terms would he have been succeeded by a Republican such as John McCain or a charismatic Democrat such as Barrack Obama?

If it had been McCain, would he have had to withdraw from a re-election challenge due to health concerns in 2016? If it had been Obama might he have won the 2016 election and, if so, would he have faced Donald Trump or another Republican in the election? Might Trump have done what he did when Obama faced re-election in 2012 and supported Romney?

In this world there seems to be little room for George W. Bush and Al Gore at least. And Donald Trump either would not yet have started a run for the Presidency or run against Obama's re-election bid.

Interesting as alternative histories are, fortunately or unfortunately, the world is as it is. Thus, even as we imagine what might have been, if we wish that things were better than they are, it behooves us to work for that change in an intelligent manner. It is, therefore, not a wasted effort to look behind the scenes of events we thought we understood but did not and, in the cold light of reality face the tasks ahead of us.

TABLE OF CONTENTS

ACKNOWLEDGEMENTS

The author wishes to thank the following individuals and organizations for their contribution both to this book and/or to the original *The Gary Hart Set-Up*. Without their assistance and counsel these books could not have been completed.

Justina Wooten	*Dr. Robert McFarland*
Paul McGuirk	*The Christic Institute*
Bill Chaney	*"George R. Walters"*
Sally Denton	*Ben Bradlee*
Tom Fiedler	*Nancy Clark*
Juan Hernandez	*Hal Wheatley*
John Blake	*Chris Wolf*
Faith Donaldson	*Nickie Lundberg*
Peter Boyles	*Tom Fiedler*

INTRODUCTION

In November of 2018, two events propelled the story of an almost forgotten, though suddenly again relevant, political figure back into the public consciousness. The political figure was former Senator and once Presidential frontrunner, Gary Hart. The events were the release of a movie based on Hart's Presidential run in the 1987 starring Hugh Jackman, called *The Frontrunner*. The other was the publication of an article entitled "Was Gary Hart Set-up?" in the November 2018 issue of the *Atlantic*.

The Frontrunner is based on the 2014 book by Matt Bai entitled *All the Truth is Out*. The *Atlantic* article was based on the deathbed confessions of Lee Atwater and his friend Raymond Strother, an official in the 1987 Hart campaign. Atwater was the campaign manager for the 1988 Bush campaign, who, according to Strother, confessed on his deathbed that he was responsible for setting Hart up in 1987, something he now regretted. Strother generally kept the information to himself until he too was dying.

Unfortunately Bai did not have knowledge of the Atwater deathbed confession prior to the publication of his book, although we suspect that he too had suspicions that there was more to the Hart affair than met the eye.
The original *The Gary Hart Set-up* written by myself and "George R. Walters", the pseudonym of a former political, intelligence and dirty trick operative, published in 1992.

The maddening thing about the Atwater confession is that when he confessed to Strother, he was so weak that he could only talk for five minutes. Five minutes was far too little time to go into detail about how the set-up was pulled off or who was or was not a willing pawn. Thus I suspect that the theories that my co-author and I put forward in 1992 are as likely as any possible scenario. With the passing of Atwater, however, much remains impossible to solidly confirm.

Without a smoking gun those of us who believed that Hart had been, at least partly set up in 1987, had to put up with a good deal of ridicule. Admittedly since "George" and I were Coloradoans it was widely suspected that at least a part of the motive for our investigation was that we were "homers." If homerism was indeed a primary motivation behind not being able to accept the "official" Hart story, it would seem ironic the most snarky review of our investigation came from *Westword*, a Denver area weekly.

Gary Hart was easily the most star-crossed Presidential candidate in this era. Consider that the press did not look into, and in some cases, actively suppressed the illicit affairs of FDR, JFK, Eisenhower, Clinton and who knows how many others. Hart was the first to have an alleged affair exposed to the national media. His campaign was also the first to have been destroyed by those revelations.

He was also the last candidate to whom revelations of that sort mattered. The Jennifer Flowers' allegations did not derail the Clinton candidacy or cost him the election. The Monica Lewinsky affair did not cost him the Presidency.

The *Access Hollywood* tape did not deny Trump the Presidency and the Stormy Daniels allegations have been an annoying but hardly fatal circumstance for the Trump Presidency. And what if Hart was more or less innocent of the charges, the tragedy is multiplied.

The first person to allege that in 1987 Gary Hart was set up was Hart himself. In the original *The Gary Hart Set-up* Hart seems certain enough of that premise:

> "The obvious answer is that I'm being set up," Gary Hart observed matter-of-factly when confronted by the *Miami Herald* reporters who had staked out his residence in Washington. The reporters chose to ignore Hart's comment and continued questioning Hart about his 'relationship' with Donna Rice and whether the two had had sex, apparently never thinking to ask why Hart felt he might be the victim of a setup that would soon destroy the very real likelihood of a Hart presidency."

Officially, Hart now claims to be less certain of a set-up and generally refuses to discuss the matter in any great detail with all but a few. If his contention that he was being set up has become less certain with time, or in any event less of an issue, Hart's limited actions in sharing information that tended to suggest either set-up or extremely suspicious circumstances seem to suggest that he still leans strongly to the set-up theory.

The notion that the course of the nation was abruptly changed in 1987 when the man that Hunter Thompson referred to as the "closest thing we have ever had to a president-in waiting," bowed out of the Presidential race as the result of a scandal that, at least to some, seemed far too convenient for Hart's competitors and enemies. That the Hart affair seemed suspicious caused a number of writers to question the accepted version. Unfortunately, those of us who believed that there was more to the Hart affair than met the eye, the evidence with just one exception was all circumstantial. To be sure, some of what we considered circumstantial evidence might have also been coincidence and/or drawing connections that could be (and were) considered overreaches.

The original *The Gary Hart Set-up* written by myself and "George R. Walters," did not lay the entire blame for the Hart debacle solely on the Bush campaign. Still, it is likely that the campaign coordinated any set-up of Hart. It also noted that the national security establishment, including the CIA, and their friends embedded in the media, had many reasons to want to derail the Hart campaign.

The exception, which eventually proved inconclusive, occurred when a team of investigative journalists commissioned by *Playboy* magazine interviewed a never identified "Federal law enforcement" official, who claimed that he had been "the one who did the job on Hart." The *Playboy* team was led by Sally Denton, author of *The Bluegrass Conspiracy* and had originally planned to publish the story in their June 1992 edition.

iv

When that did not occur, *Playboy* spokesmen stated that they had lost confidence in "the Fed."

To avoid confusion, what follows is a combination of the new information, gleaned primarily although not exclusively from the *Atlantic* and *All the Truth is Out* regarding the Hart affair and is presented in the unnumbered chapters "Vindication: The Atwater Deathbed Confession," "The Tragic Frontrunner," and "The Mysterious Turnberry Women." Following that are extensive excerpts from *The Gary Hart Set-Up* published in 1992 in numbered chapters. Following these are letters from Gary Hart, Ben Bradlee, the legendary Executive Editor of the *Washington Post*, who presided over the *Post*'s Watergate coverage, and Playboy magazine. Following those are the three articles written by the author and published by the now defunct Denver area weekly *Metropolitan Accent*, that dealt directly and indirectly with the Hart affair, *A New Book Asks: Was Gary Hart Set-Up, Spies on the Front Range* and *Blood Moon Rising*.

VINDICATION? THE ATWATER DEATHBED CONFESSION

VINDICATION!!! AFTER 26 YEARS OF RIDICULE, LEE ATWATER'S DEATHBED CONVICTION CONFIRMS THAT GARY HART WAS SET UP

In 1992 together with a former Republican "opposition researcher" officially, and dirty tricks specialist unofficially, using the pseudonym "George Walters," I wrote a book entitled *The Gary Hart Set-Up* that cited the curious circumstances and "startling series of coincidences" that caused us to come to the conclusion that the Hart campaign was derailed by political dirty tricks that seemed to have the fingerprints of then Vice-President George Herbert Walker Bush all over them. In 1993, after many other publications either rejected it or oddly went out of business just prior to publication, I wrote an article for a then Denver area weekly, *Metropolitan Accent*, that covered much of the same terrain. It would not be until 2018 that the evidence for the Hart set-up would amount to anything other than some very suspicious circumstances.

In November of 2018, the *Atlantic Monthly* contained an article by James Fallows entitled "Was Gary Hart Set Up?," which asked " What are we to make of the deathbed confession of the political operative and 1988 Bush Campaign manager, Lee Atwater, newly revealed, that he staged the events that brought down the Democratic candidate in 1987?"

For those of us not old enough to have lived through those times or remembered them with any precision, the article noted that Atwater had been a most effective and brutal operative who had helped Bush become President, including using the infamous Willie Horton attack ads, which played "leveraged the issue of race..." against the eventual Democratic nominee, Michael Dukakis. According to the *Atlantic* "The explicit message of the commercial was that, as governor of Massachusetts, Dukakis had been soft on crime by offering furloughs to convicted murderers; Horton ran away while on furlough and then committed new felonies, including rape. The implicit message was the menace posed by hulking, scowling black men—like the Willie Horton who was shown in the commercial."

Unfortunately for Atwater, he was not to live long enough to fully enjoy the fruits of his efforts for as the article pointed out "In the spring of 1990, after he had helped the first George Bush reach the presidency, the political consultant Lee Atwater learned that he was dying. Atwater, who had just turned 39 and was the head of the Republican National Committee, had suffered a seizure while at a political fund-raising breakfast and had been diagnosed with an inoperable brain tumor. In a year he was dead."

Apparently Atwater had significant regrets and "put some of that year to use making amends," including publicly apologizing to Dukakis "for the 'naked cruelty' of the Willie Horton ad." Privately, he told Raymond Strother, "…his Democratic competitor and counterpart…" that "…he was sorry for how he had torpedoed Gary Hart's chances of becoming President." Strother had been Hart's media consultant during Hart's 1984 campaign that "…gave former Vice President Mondale a scare…(and that)…As the campaign for the 1988 nomination geared up, Strother planned to play a similar role."

Again for those of us either not old enough to have remembered or to have forgotten the political situation in early 1987 Fallows explains that "the Hart campaign had an air of likelihood if not inevitability that is difficult to imagine in retrospect. After Mondale's landslide defeat by Ronald Reagan in 1984, Hart had become the heir apparent and best hope to lead the party back to the White House.

Fallows notes that he had met Hart previously, written about him in a number of *Atlantic* articles that led to his 1981 book, *National Defense*. Fallows stated that he had stayed in touch with Hart and "respected his work and his views." He points out that despite Hart's lead in the 1988 Democratic field and over Bush, the presumptive Republican nominee, Hart was vulnerable to "…the press's suggestion that something about him was hidden, excessively private or 'unknowable.'

The presumed Republican nominee was Bush, Reagan's vice president, who was seen at the time, like many vice presidents before him, as a lackluster understudy.

Since the FDR–Truman era, no party had won three straight presidential elections, which the Republicans would obviously have to do if Bush were to succeed Reagan."

Among other things, this was a way of alluding to suspicions of extramarital affairs – a theme in most accounts of that campaign, including Matt Bai's 2014 *All the Truth is Out* (which comes to the big screen in November 2018 in the form of *The Frontrunner* starring Hugh Jackman as Hart). Still as Bai wrote in his book, "Everyone agreed: it was Hart's race to lose."

As for the curious circumstance of a hardline Republican activist and dirty trickster choosing an equally hardline Democratic activist to hear his deathbed confession, Fallows explains that "Strother and Atwater had the mutually respectful camaraderie of highly skilled rivals. 'Lee and I were friends,' Strother told me when I spoke with him by phone recently. 'We'd meet after campaigns and have coffee, talk about why I did what I did and why he did what he did what he did."

One of those post-campaign conversations occurred shortly after the 1988 presidential race but it was not until Atwater realized that he was dying in 1991 that he phoned Strother to discuss "one more detail of that campaign."

According to Strother, "Atwater had the strength to talk for only five minutes. 'It wasn't a conversation,' Strother said when I spoke with him recently. 'There weren't any pleasantries. It was like he was working down a checklist, and he had something he had to tell me before he died.'" According to Strother, what Atwater wanted to impart to him was the "...episode that triggered Hart's withdrawal from the race, which became known as the *Monkey Business* affair, had not been bad luck but a trap." At the time of the *Monkey Business* affair Strother remembers that he thought "...there was something fishy about the whole thing..." After Atwater told Strother "I did it!...I fixed Hart" Strother realized that his long held suspicions were true.

Although Strother largely kept the account of his conversation with Atwater to himself, he "....discreetly mentioned the conversation to some journalists and other colleagues, but not to Gary Hart." In retrospect, Strother remarks that, "I probably should have told him at the time...(but)...It was a judgment call, and I didn't see the point in involving him in another controversy." Additionally, "Strother realized, he had no proof, and probably never would. Atwater was dead. Although Hart did not run in later elections, he was busy and productive: He had earned a doctorate in politics at Oxford, had published many books, and had co-chaired the Hart-Rudman commission which memorably warned the incoming president in 2001, George W. Bush to prepare for a terrorist attack on American soil."

Ironically, however, just as Atwater's grim prognosis caused him to confess to Strother late in 2017, Strother learned that "…the prostate cancer he had been treated for a dozen years ago, had returned and spread, and that he might not have long to live…Strother began traveling to see people he had known and worked with, to say goodbye. One of his stops was Colorado, where he had a meal with Gary Hart."

During that meal Hart "…asked Strother to think about the high points of the (1988) campaign, and its lows…" Strother responded that "…a whole list of 'coincidences' (involved with the *Monkey Business* affair) that had been on my mind for 30 years, and that could lead a reasonable person to think none of it happened by accident…I know you were set up."

When a surprised Hart asked Strother "…how he could be so certain….Strother recalled his long-ago talk with Atwater and Atwater's claim that the whole *Monkey Business* weekend had occurred at his direction." Hart then opined that such a plan would have had to involve "…contriving an invitation from Broadhurst for Hart to come on a boat ride, when Hart intended to be working on a speech. Ensuring that young women would be invited aboard. Arranging for the Broadhurst boat Hart thought he would be boarding, with some memorable name, to be unavailable – so the group would have to switch to another boat, *Monkey Business*. Persuading Broadhurst to 'forget' to check with customs clearance in Bimini before closing time, so that the boat 'unexpectedly' had to stay overnight there. And, according to Hart, organizing an opportunistic photo-grab."

According to Hart while waiting on the pier, Donna Rice friend Lynn Armandt, "…made a gesture to Miss Rice, and she immediately came over and sat on my lap. Miss Armandt (then) took the picture (which then famously was featured on the front page of the *National Enquirer* and subsequently all over the world). The whole thing took less than five seconds.…It was clearly staged, but it was used after the fact to prove that some intimacy existed." Despite the passage of time, any challenge to the explanation that the failure of the Hart campaign in 1988 was the result of an extra-marital affair that happened to get exposed by an unbiased press and good journalism, was likely to met with some resistance, especially from the journalists involved. James "Jim" Savage, who was on the *Miami Herald*'s team of reporters that stalked Hart, responded to Fallows article with a letter to the editor of *The Atlantic* dated October 20, 2018 entitled "Gary Hart Was Not Set Up."

Savage introduced himself as "…the *Miami Herald's* investigations editor who helped report and edit the 1987 stories that uncovered Gary Hart's relationship with Donna Rice…" Savage and the strange behavior of the *Miami Herald* in the Hart affair and on other occasions is mentioned in the original *The Gary Hart Set-up* in the chapter entitled "A Startling Series of Coincidences."

Following the author's 1991 request for information concerning the role of The *Miami Herald* in the Hart affair, on September 18, 1991 the *Herald* replied with a 16 page account of the newspaper's activities that made clear that this was their "unbending final position on the matter."

The account raised a number of questions and seemed to contradict itself on basic questions including differing accounts of who first received the anonymous tip that set off the *Herald* investigation.

Savage's letter, entitled "Gary Hart was not Set-Up" contended that "…from my personal knowledge of the facts that *The Atlantic*'s article contains serious factual errors."

Savage cited two instances of what he considered "serious factual errors." The first (if entirely true) threw some significant doubt about whether or not William Broadhurst, who set up the *Monkey Business* voyage, was deliberately acting against Hart's interests in doing so. Savage declared that "The truth is the late Mr. Broadhurst did everything short of violence trying to prevent the *Herald*'s investigations team from publishing the first story about the scandal."

Specifically, "Reporters Tom Fiedler, Jim McGee, and I were preparing that story on deadline after interviewing Hart about his relationship with the young woman from Miami when Broadhurst phoned our hotel room in Washington."

Savage goes on to state that "Broadhurst insisted that he had invited the Miami woman and a friend to Washington and any story we wrote would unfairly portray Hart's relationship….We included Broadhurst's defense of Hart in that first story."

8

Besides, Savage insisted, "Broadurst died recently and can't defend himself," perhaps suggesting that anyone suggesting Broadhurst's involvement in anti-Hart conspiracy is not only speaking ill of the recently deceased, and an all too convenient unknowable to assist the conspiracy theory.

Savage also insisted that Donna Rice had no deliberate role in any anti-Hart conspiracy, but cited no evidence other than his "….firsthand knowledge…." without citing any specific examples, but nonetheless insisting that "…*The Atlantic* should publish a correction and an apology to Ms. Rice…"

Savage did not address or acknowledge the Atwater confession. He simply ignored it. Nor did Savage acknowledge that Broadhurst's and perhaps even Donna Rice's role in an anti-Hart conspiracy could well have been unknowing, just as could have been the role of the *Miami Herald*. It might also have been possible that even if Broadhurst had knowingly set up Hart, he was now remorseful.

At least Savage did not respond to Atwater's deathbed confession the way one wag responded to E. Howard Hunt's deathbed confession of being a part of the plot to assassinate President Kennedy. The wag, apparently unfamiliar with social injunction that it is good manners to avoid speaking ill of the dead, disputed Hunt's confession, referring to Hunt as a serial liar. But lying on his deathbed? That would seem to be an unusual commitment to disseminating falsehoods.

For evidence the wag asserted that Hunt had planted false evidence in the National Archives that said that JFK had ordered the overthrow and execution of South Vietnamese President Diem, and lied about his whereabouts on day of JFK's assassination. Curiously, however, the wag apparently believed that Hunt was one of the so-called "tramps" arrested near the grassy knoll, and even thought that Hunt might have been a second gunman.

Fallows responded to Savage's letter declaring that *"The details of the Miami Herald's handling of the Gary Hart–Donna Rice case were explicitly not the topic of my article. The literature on the topic is too vast and contradictory to set out, even in a magazine article many times longer than the one I wrote."*

Despite the fact that the Herald's handling of the affair was not his primary focus, Fallows notes that "…Over the decades, many of those involved in the Herald's decision to send reporters for a stakeout of Gary Hart's house in Washington have stoutly defended the public and journalistic interests they believed they served in doing so, and the care they took in choosing this course. Mr. Savage, who was involved in those decisions, defends them in his note."

However, Fallows notes that serious questions about the press handling of the matter remain. "Over the decades, many people not involved in the choices have debated these same aspects: whether the Herald exercised sufficient care in pursuing the tip it received and what the consequences were of the way it (and, separately, The Washington Post, then handled the "scandal" of Hart's possible affairs. Back in 1987, the journalist John Judis offered a skeptical and negative assessment of the Herald's and The Post's approaches in the Columbia Journalism Review. Matt Bai's 2014 book about the episode, All the Truth Is Out, is about the way that coverage of Hart became the moment when 'politics went tabloid' and changed both politics and journalism for the worse."

Regardless, Fallows goes on to explain that the article's true focus was not the role of the press but that "It was about the circumstances in which Hart, Donna Rice, another woman named Lynn Armandt, and Billy Broadhurst got together on a boat in the first place, which led to the tip the Herald later received. Broadhurst, a lobbyist and fixer, was by all accounts a man of many faces. I have no reason to doubt Mr. Savage's report of the Herald's dealings with him. Other people who dealt with him firsthand, and have spoken with me about him, have offered much less positive perspectives." Hart himself stopped speaking to Broadhurst years earlier.

While new revelations, especially the Atwater and Strother deathbed confessions, provide new evidence that those of us who saw a hidden hand behind the destruction of the Hart campaign, they do not conclusively prove the case. Fallows acknowledges that noting that, "the story was careful to present new information as a possibility—as another way of thinking about a consequential moment in modern political history. The headline of the story was not 'Gary Hart Was Set Up.' Instead it asked, 'Was Gary Hart Set Up?'"

11

Still, Fallows notes that while the truth in this case may be unprovable or even unknowable the questions asked are not insignificant. Fallows asks "What if Lee Atwater's deathbed admission to his colleague and competitor, Raymond Strother, was actually true? What if the Monkey Business disaster was not just a catastrophic error by Hart but a setup plan?"

Fallows wonders aloud how history was changed or might have different had the Hart campaign succeeded writing that "No one can know whether Gary Hart would have gone on to the nomination or the presidency if this scandal hadn't erupted when it did; or whether some other scandal might have ensued if this one hadn't; or whether Hart, like Bill Clinton after him, to say nothing of Donald Trump, might have ridden out the scandal coverage if he'd decided just to brazen his way through; or whether Michael Dukakis might have risen to the nomination even if Hart had stayed in the race; or whether George H. W. Bush was destined for election anyway; or a thousand other imponderables. The point of the story was: History is full of counterfactual what ifs, which by definition are unknowable, and the Atwater-Strother-Hart series of conversations adds another unknowable but provocative what if to the list."

As far as Savage's insistence that Fallows and *the Atlantic* owe Donna Rice an apology Fallows responds that "...I disagree. First, the article does not say what Mr. Savage thinks it does. Lee Atwater told Raymond Strother (according to Strother) that he, Atwater, was behind the whole episode.

12

Necessarily, Billy Broadhurst would have to have been involved as well. Who else might have been, and what witting or unwitting roles the other main figures (including Donna Rice) might have played, Atwater did not tell Strother, and Strother did not claim to me.

Donna Rice Hughes presumably knows more than other still-living figures about this incident. I sent her many messages asking for a chance to talk and explaining what I wanted to ask. I know that she received at least some of them. She chose not to reply to repeated requests, which is her right and is entirely understandable. But it is not the occasion for an apology on my side."

THE MOST TRAGIC FRONTRUNNER

Some have taken the position that while Hart may or may not have been set up, the conduct of the media "feeding frenzy," that proved fatal to his campaign, not only deprived the nation of what might have been enlightened leadership, but also paved the way to the increasingly destructive political discourse that has plagued the nation since 1987.

Perhaps the best example is Matt Bai's 2014 book *All The Truth is Out: The Week Politics Went Tabloid.* Scheduled for a November 2018 release is the movie based on the book, entitled *The Frontrunner*, starring Hugh Jackman as Gary Hart.

In his preface Bai acknowledges Hart set-up believer, Richard Ben Kramer and his book *What It Takes –The Way to the White House*:

From: ***ALL THE TRUTH IS OUT: THE WEEK POLITICS WENT TABLOID***
"One of the first people I called after I decided to write this book in 2009, was Richard Ben Kramer. This was not a call I made lightly. I had, by this time, been writing about politics for *The New York Times Magazine* for the better part of a decade, so I was not exactly a journalistic unknown. But Richard was in a different category altogether. He was one of the greatest nonfiction writers of this or any age, and his seminal, 1,047 page chronicle of the 1988 presidential campaign - *What It Takes – The Way to the White House*, was arguably the greatest and most

ambitious work of political journalism in American history."

Bai never quite comes out and states a belief in a set-up of Hart. He seemed to hold the same "agnostic" belief in the conspiracy that Hart himself had expressed, years later. After all his book's publication date is 2014, four years before the Atwater deathbed confession was reported. Yet he did believe that "I had come to believe that there was something misunderstood and significant in the story of Gary Hart. I thought the forces that led to Hart's undoing were more complicated and consequential, looking back now, than anybody had really appreciated at the time...."

Although Bai stayed true to his instincts, he faced the same self-doubts and ridicule that others who investigated the Hart setup faced before him "...I confessed that I had begun to doubt myself, however. Almost invariably, when I mentioned the idea (for the book) to colleagues and friends in Washington, they reacted as if I might be teasing them –as if I had just said I was going to write my next book about bird migration or the Treaty of Westphalia...."

That was not to say, however, that Bai did not take note of the mysterious circumstances surrounding the Hart affair, even the most disturbing. For example, in addition to the suspicions that Hart loyalists had concerning William Broadhurst's role in the *Monkey Business* affair. Bai also took some note of the murder of Don Aronow, the speedboat manufacturer, friend of George Bush, as well as Donnie Soffer (according to *Blue* Thunder, the "employer" of Donna Rice), and who was about to be called before a federal grand jury.

15

Aronow was murdered gangland style just months before the Hart debacle.

The Atlantic article never made mention Aronow.

When two inmates doing a life sentence for other crimes confessed to the Aronow killing, it seemed too convenient for some. Still, most considered the Aronow murder peripheral to, rather than integral to any anti-Hart conspiracy. Bai and Cramer are apparently not so sure:

From *All the Truth is Out*
"*Monkey Business,* as it turned out, was owned by a guy named Donald Soffer, who had bought, and developed most of Turnberry Isle. Soffer's friends included the speedboat magnate Donald Aronow, who was in turn a friend and supporter of George H. W. Bush's. In February 1987, not two months before Hart stepped foot on *Monkey Business*, Aronow was gunned down in a Mafia style execution.

In *Blue Thunder,* a sensational investigative book on the Aronow murder published in 1990, journalists Thomas Burdick and Charlene Mitchell alleged that Lynn Armandt, the Donna Rice friend who snapped the photo of Rice sitting on Hart's lap, had been connected to Soffer and to people in the narcotics trade, and they reported that federal agents had found a sheath of Hart's stump speeches in the safe of Ben Kramer, another local syndicate figure, after he was arrested.

What did all these disparate clues add up to? That was anyone's guess.

16

Hart would never go as far as to say he believed in a conspiracy, but he didn't discount it, either; he declared himself 'agnostic' on the question. 'It was either the most unbelievable tragedy of errors,' he once told me, 'or it was a setup. And no one's ever going to know.'

Once, an old supporter sent Hart, without comment, a video making the rounds on YouTube, which Hart forwarded to me. The video featured a long interview with Chip Tatum, who claimed, believably, to have been a high-level black ops agent with the CIA in the late 1980s, and who disappeared in 1998. Tatum said he had worked with Oliver North and carried out orders from then Vice President Bush, including some to assassinate foreign nationals. About an hour into the video, he said he had been asked by the Republican administration to 'neutralize' Hart's campaign, and while he refused to take such covert action against an American citizen, he assumed someone else had accepted the assignment.

(Tatum's allegation was undercut by his assertion that agents had subsequently taped Hart's affair with Rice and leaked it to the press, which never actually occurred). Tatum has also claimed that he had also been ordered to "neutralize" Ross Perot. Still, Tatum's allegations cannot be dismissed out of hand, and the fact he has apparently either been forcibly or voluntarily disappeared seems to added credibility to them.

JOE KELSO
The fact that alleged "high level black ops CIA agent" Tatum disappeared without a trace, brought to mind the case of Joe Kelso.

17

Kelso also claimed to be a high level black ops CIA contract agent and disappeared in the late 1980s and whose name even appeared in the Oliver North diary. To my knowledge the only articles and books that talked extensively about Kelso were ones I had a hand in. Our primary informant on the Kelso matter was a Boulder, Colorado doctor named Robert McFarland, who ran the Boulder Methadone clinic:

From *The Gary Hart Set-Up*

"McFarland had a wealth of information and stated that he was willing to go on the record concerning conversations that he was involved in. One such conversation was with the Boulder Deputy District Attorney in 1985, in which the Deputy D.A. told McFarland that Boulder did not have the resources to pursue a comprehensive drug investigation in the aftermath of the heroin lab discovery (on the premises of a top secret military contractor in Boulder). An even more unsettling conversation involved McFarland, McGuirk (the former heroin addict who informed McFarland about the existence of heroin lab), and Joe Kelso, (nearly universally acknowledged as a CIA agent), who had been arrested for selling missiles to Iraq and is mentioned in the Iran-Contra investigations.

McFarland began to suspect that Kelso was something of an assassin and brought up the subject of the unsolved assassination of Swedish Prime Minister Olof Palme, wondering aloud if the murder might have been carried out by the agency.

Indeed it was, Kelso agreed, adding that he had been in Amsterdam during the planning of the Palme assassination. Olof Palme was assassinated by an unknown gunman on March 3, 1986. A composite drawing of the suspect received wide circulation before a suspect was arrested on March 13. The suspect was released on March 20, 1986 and the Swedish government acknowledged that the assassination remained a mystery. Kelso told McFarland that he planned to go back to the CIA soon, hinting that he was concerned about the welfare of his family. In fact, Kelso has never been heard from since.

As an aside, on the Peter Boyles radio talk show in the early 1990s, I was discussing an article I had written for the now defunct *Metropolitan Accent*, entitled 'Spies on the Front Range,' which detailed my findings concerning Kelso and other Colorado based 'spooks' including a former Luftwaffe ace who flew for Air America in Southeast Asia and possibly connected to black projects funding via the Savings and Loan scandal named Heinreich Rupp.

One caller stated that he was a neighbor of Rupp's in Aurora and that he had been told that Rupp 1. was an unrepentant Nazi and, in a revelation that gave both Peter and myself a good laugh, 2. so hated George Bush that when Bush was in Colorado, the Secret Service would take Rupp for an airplane ride that concluded only after Bush was out of town. To my astonishment Rupp himself, or someone credibly pretending to be Rupp, complete with strong German accent, called in to the show.

Although I thought this would be a good opportunity to ask Rupp questions that he alone would know the answer to, Rupp was clearly evasive on most points. One point he was not evasive on, however, was the suspicion that Kelso was no longer among the living. Kelso, he remarked 'had made his own funeral.'"

While Bai proposes no conspiracy theory that involves Aronow, and had the disadvantage of not knowing about the Atwater confession prior to the publication of his book in 2014, he does wonder aloud about William Broadhurst's deliberate or unknowing role in any anti-Hart conspiracy along the same lines as Fallows and *the Atlantic*:

Broadhurst speculation in *All the Truth is Out*

"In *What it Takes,* Cramer alluded to the "true believers" in Hart's camp who would posit, in the months that followed, that everything was Broadhurst's fault, and not Hart's – that it was Billy number two who stupidly set up the cruise in the first place, and who kept them in Bimini, and who couldn't just let the women walk off the boat and out of Hart's life forever. Decades later, Billy Shore would clearly remember a moment in an airport holding room in Iowa, just a few days before Hart met Broadhurst and the two women for a second engagement in Washington. Shore had a stack of those old pink message slips that used to say "While you were out," on them and leafing through the pile, he handed Hart the one from Broadhurst, since he knew Hart would want to return the call. Then Shore left the room for a moment…When he returned, Hart was on the phone and Shore could only hear his part of the conversation.

I don't know Bill, I really have to work on that speech this weekend, Shore recalled Hart saying, or something to that effect. (Hart had a major economics address scheduled for that following Tuesday). *I appreciate the thought, but I'm not sure it's a good idea.* Shore was too kind to blatantly point the finger at anyone all these years later, but the implication of the memory was clear: it was Broadhurst who engineered a reunion between Hart and Donna Rice that weekend in Washington, and he must have brought Rice over to see Hart despite the boss's stated reluctance. In the many years after Broadhurst disappeared back to the bayou, never to be heard from in Washington again, this sentiment would intensify and darken, to the point where some Hart loyalists entertained elaborate – if not entirely implausible – conspiracy theories. Could someone have paid Billy Broadhurst or Lynn Armandt to set Hart up? Did the Republicans, whose soon to be nominee was a former CIA director, want to get Hart out of the way, the way Nixon's guys managed to knock off Ed Muskie with a dirty trick fifteen years earlier? Did the Mafia, still rattled by disclosures about their ties to Kennedy in the Church Committee report, want to make sure Hart didn't get to the White House? Hart had been, after all, the committee's most persistent in questioning the Warren Commission's official report on the Kennedy assassination, and he had publicly promised, several times, to reopen the investigation as president."

21

THE MYSTERIOUS TURNBERRY WOMEN

The real Donna Rice (Hughes) is elusive. She has been called a born-again Christian who dated a Southern Baptist minister and attended Billy Graham crusades. Yet *Blue Thunder* called her one of "Donnie's party girls," and she posed semi-topless for an ad for a Miami bar. Now she seems to have come back to the faith, crusading for internet safety for children and combating pornography with her group "Enough is enough."

She was called a "political groupie," but others say she had no interest in politics whatever. She has been called extremely intelligent (she graduated Phi Beta Kappa from the University of South Carolina as a biology major), yet Dana Weems, another of the Turnberry women, whom the *New York Times* reported was the *Herald's* Hart affair tipster reportedly called her "empty-headed."

She has alternately courted and shunned publicity, appearing on *Miami Vice, One Life to Live* and giving early interviews to the press in the days immediately following the *Miami Herald* article. Yet shortly thereafter she dropped out of sight for seven years, reappearing as the spokeswoman for "No Excuses" jeans. In 1994, the same year she married her husband, she became the spokesperson for "Enough is enough."

Without being specific about what sort of "unhealthy lifestyle" she is talking about, she blames a date rape by an older pageant official (she was Miss South Carolina World pageant winner), as being "…the turning point in my life, the catalyst that propelled me further into an unhealthy lifestyle." Ironically, she is now an outspoken supporter of President Trump, the former owner of the Miss USA and Miss Universe pageants, who bragged about walking into the dressing rooms of the pageant.

Lynn Armandt, the woman described by *Blue Thunder* as being the supervisor of "Donnie's party girls," also must have been traumatized when her husband was apparently murdered in a hail of bullets, although his body was never found. The notion that Armandt had taken the "Donnie's party girls" job out of compulsion seems to be countered by the fact that shortly before she went completely underground, she declared that despite the $25,000 she received from *People* magazine for the photo of Rice on Hart's lap, the Hart affair had "ruined her life."

From *Blue Thunder*

"Joey Ippolito also shared a mistress with Don Aronow at Turnberry, recalls Don Soffer. 'Donnie,' the developer of Turnberry, is perhaps best known for his yacht, "Monkey Business." He and Aronow were very close, Suzanne recalls, "Don Aronow came over a lot."

Soffer enjoyed the titillating gossip that surrounded his creation and its unrepentantly chauvinistic atmosphere. He, himself christened one of his boats "Be Right Back" – his favorite saying to his ex-wife before he'd disappear for several days. He employed small-time models like Donna Rice and Lynn Armandt and beautiful young women, nicknamed "Donnie's girls," as Turnberry hostesses.

Armandt was the manager of these 'party girls.' Their job responsibilities were open ended."

The authors of *Blue Thunder* write that the Aronow murder was "apparently unrelated" to the Gary Hart debacle. However, they then list circumstances that might cause one to question that assumption to the extent that it seems that the use of the phrase "apparently unrelated" is possibly used to cover real suspicions:

"A titillating piece of information had come my way while looking into the Aronow story. Although apparently unrelated to the murder it reinforced the omnipresence of the mob and its infiltration into all aspects of society. When the feds busted Ben Kramer, they discovered originals of Gary Hart's stump speeches in Ben's Fort Apache safe. Somehow a Lansky, Inc. drug kingpin had gotten possession of a presidential contender's papers. At the time that Hart was blown out of the presidential waters, he had been the Democratic front runner. The rest of the Democratic contenders seemed to have little chance of knocking Hart off the winning path.

On the Republican side was George Bush, the heir apparent to the Reagan era. Bush was considered a weak candidate; even Reagan had expressed doubts about his loyal veep's presidential fortitude. It looked as if the Democrats might capture the White House for the first time in eight years.

Suddenly 'Snow White,' as Hart was dubbed by the press, was devastatingly and humiliatingly knocked out of contention.

With the Democrats' strong front runner gone, the party was divided among the 'Seven Dwarfs,' the remaining Democratic candidates. The precarious unity was gone, and a fractious campaign ensued with no one able to amass the strength Hart once commanded.

Despite Gail Sheehy's famous 'psycho-political' article in *Vanity Fair* about Hart, there may be more behind the story than simply the tale of a man whose rigid religious upbringing forced him to punish himself by self-destructing. A closer look at the Hart debacle reveals an interesting panorama played out behind the highly publicized story.

Lynn Armandt, the woman who brought Gary Hart down, had worked for a long time at Turnberry Isle before the infamous "Monkey Business" trip in May 1987. Don Soffer, the developer and manager of the resort, had made her head of 'Donnie's party girls' – which some cynics likened to high priced call girls. He also provided her with free floor space to sell bikinis. (Turnberry shops are considered some of the most expensive retail space in Miami). In all, an extremely lucrative position for a woman with her background.

She and Donna Rice, another of Donnie's girls, were very good friends. The two women lived in upscale neighboring condominiums not far from Turnberry and Thunderboat Alley. As Donnie's girls, Armandt and Rice made money, 'dated' wealthy and famous men and had entrée to Miami's high flying lifestyle.

After the incident, Rice supposedly ended her association with Armandt, angered over the 'betrayal.' Or so she told Barbara Walters in a 20/20 television interview.

But people at Turnberry saw the two women together often after the Hart affair. A maintenance man at Rice's condo saw them sunbathing at the pool frequently both before and after the 20/20 piece. 'They were laughing and joking and were the best of girlfriends,' he said; 'Nothing changed.'

As the scrutiny of the scandal continued unabated, Armandt moved to New York and then went underground. She was castigated as a money hungry woman who sold out her friend and brought down a presidential candidate for a handful of dollars. But if she had been so inclined, why not blow the cover on some of the other celebrities who cavorted at the resort over the years? The resort's client roster included a long list of powerful and celebrated men. Some whose often compromising activities there would have been ideal fodder for the gossip rags.

A street smart woman such as Armandt knew she would become a pariah among Turnberry clientele and her relationship with her boss and benefactor would be severed if she published the secret life of any patron. Armandt also knew that some of the Turnberry boys could play a rough game. If it ever slipped her mind, she only had to remember what happened to her drug-smuggling husband. The last trace of him was a bloody bullet riddled car and a piece of paper containing the telephone number of Turnberry patron Ben Kramer.

Gary Hart had already been to Turnberry before the 'Monkey Business' incident, despite his denials. When he returned in May 1987, a 'set up' may have been arranged with Armandt being directed at every step of the way. One fed who has investigated Turnberry (he alleges that the 29 story condominium is 'mobbed up from the 29th floor down') agrees with the notion that the Hart affair was masterminded by OC interests."

Dana Weems, was the relatively unknown Turnberry woman until recently when Matt Bai outed her as the *Miami Herald* tipster in his book and his article in the *Sunday New York Times*. Interestingly, when the *Herald* reported his *Times* article it left the impression that Weems was still being coy about being the tipster. In his book Bai quotes Weems as unequivocally admitting that she was the tipster. He also noted that Weems was jealous of and did not particularly seem to like Donna Rice.

Weems who was a clothing designer, and model, sold some of her wares in the shop run by Lynn Armandt. Bai quotes Weems as stating that she didn't think Rice was as attractive a model as herself, maybe "good enough for commercials, I guess." Weems also expressed a great annoyance with Rice. At the time of the affair Rice speculated that Weems was the tipster.

Weems motivations for contacting the *Herald* apparently had little to do with a concern for the well-being of Rice.

When Weems called the *Herald* she reportedly declared that she was a "liberal democrat," as though it was somehow important that she declare that she had no political axe to grind. She also asked the *Herald* how much it paid for pictures, suggesting a possible connection to the Armandt staged photo. In the end Armandt sold the Monkey Business photos to *People* for $25,000.

Weems told Bai that MS had confined her to a wheelchair. On the other hand an interview with Donna Rice conducted four years ago, demonstrated that Rice was still an uncommonly attractive and young looking woman. While Rice has aged wonderfully well, most of the other actors involved have not.

What follows now are the most pertinent excerpts from the original *The Gary Hart Set-up* and any more recent findings and updates that shed any light on the original book and, of course, what actually occurred in 1987. Published in 1992, *The Gary Hart Set-up* briefly sold well at local Denver area bookstores, especially Denver's unique mega bookstore, the Tattered Cover. As time went on and no new revelations came to light, the book went out of print, although there was a brief period when someone was offering a copy of the book on the net for an amazing $650.

PROLOGUE TO THE ORIGINAL *THE GARY HART SET-UP*

"…Among the subjects discussed for the first time are a possible assassination attempt aimed at Hart in 1983, the existence of a 'second Donna Rice' and/or a 'second Gary Hart,' which appeared on a videotape run on the CBS network that has subsequently become unavailable, and inconsistencies in the accounts of the *Miami Herald* including two versions of the phone calls from a secret informer were received.

…Also revealed are the stories of two people who may have lost their lives because they knew too much about the Hart set-up….The text also explores the ease with which political 'dirty tricks' can be carried out during a presidential campaign as well as the CIA's role in election rigging, domestic covert operations in violation of the agency's charter…other attempted and discovered CIA attempts at sexual blackmail operations, and manipulation of the media and propaganda assets – a term the Agency uses to refer to its media operatives.

The Gary Hart Set-up also brings to light the incomprehensible actions that were undertaken by the *Washington Post*, which, in effect, used the contents of a never released private detective's report to blackmail Hart into withdrawing from the race, the possible intelligence operative cover of Donna Rice and the drug dealing connections of both Rice and her friend Lynn Armandt. …Also revealed are the stories of two people who may have lost their lives because they knew too much about the Hart set-up….The text also explores the ease with which political 'dirty tricks' can be carried out during a presidential campaign as well as the CIA's role in election rigging, domestic covert operations in violation of the agency's charter…other attempted and discovered CIA attempts at sexual blackmail operations, and manipulation of the media and propaganda assets – a term the Agency uses to refer to its media operatives.

FROM THE ORIGINAL *THE GARY HART SET-UP*

CHAPTER ONE: DIRTY TRICKS

"The obvious answer is that I'm being set up," Gary Hart observed matter-of-factly when confronted by the *Miami Herald* reporters who had staked out his residence in Washington. The reporters chose to ignore Hart's comment and continued questioning Hart about his 'relationship' with Donna Rice and whether the two had had sex, apparently never thinking to ask why Hart felt he might be the victim of a setup that would soon destroy the very real likelihood of a Hart presidency.

….An Iowa poll conducted the month prior to Hart's withdrawal showed that Hart had the support of two thirds of all Democrats and had a 23 percent lead over George Bush in a theoretical match-up….After Hart's exit, what remained was a Democratic field that the press dubbed the 'seven dwarfs.' Although Michael Dukakis easily went on to win the Democratic nomination, his lack of charisma and the 'Willie Horton' negative ads spelled a landslide defeat for him….

…The 1992 election seemed to be another good chance for a Democrat…because of …the declining economy under Bush, the Savings and Loan scandal, Bush's health scares…Danforth Quayle…et.al. Early on Bill Clinton…became the …frontrunner…However, just prior to the New Hampshire primary, Clinton like Hart, became the subject of a growing media firestorm of accusations of sexual dalliances. Those familiar with the Hart affair may notice the striking similarity to the same sorts of rumors which appeared in *Newsweek* just weeks before the Rice affair and which set the stage for the media blitzkrieg that followed. Soon after the womanizing rumors, Hart's campaign was over. However, the allegations only wounded Clinton's campaign – they did not put an end to it. Why were the rumors of an extramarital affair alone not enough to (also) ruin Clinton's campaign? Perhaps there was more to the Hart affair than met the eye.

Most Americans and nearly all the press seemed to accept that the Hart-Rice affair was nothing more than it appeared to be on the surface: a case of apparent (if incomprehensible) lust on the part of a well-known politician for a young "political groupie." Hart's judgment was attacked perhaps more than his morals and once the scandal became the grist for late night comedians serious discussion ended.

Why the affair was so readily accepted at face value is not clear. Very little is really known for certain about the affair. Could it have been, as Senator Hart contended, that he was set up? In order to begin to fairly investigate this proposition, the sufficient motive, means and opportunity for such an idea to be plausible all need to be analyzed. Certainly a motive to derail the Hart campaign would be present in the plans of his competitors for the Presidency, both Democratic and Republican, since he wa, at the time of the Rice affair, far and away the odds-on favorite to be in the Oval Office in January of 1989.

There were other entities who might have felt threatened by a Hart presidency – entities who may have had the ability and the motivation to set up Hart. Hart had been an outspoken critic of the Warren Commission, a critic of the CIA's covert operations and opponent of the "secret war" against the Sandinistas in Nicaragua in the 1980s. Any major opposition to the Nicaraguan war and covert operations might also have had the effect of ruining a highly lucrative enterprise, of which the CIA may have been either a main force or an important partner.

Therefore, the intelligence community could also easily have had a motive.

Means for the set-up could be a sophisticated covert capability coupled with strategic access to key elements of the media and a number of operatives and/or dupes in the right places at the right times. The most likely possessors of this sort of means are the covert activities branches of various intelligence agencies, most likely the CIA. It had already been demonstrated that the CIA was no fan of the idea of a Hart presidency. A CIA wish to aid the campaign of former CIA director Bush by carrying out operations against the Hart campaign is also a possibility.

Further there is some evidence that intelligence professionals within the government aided the Reagan campaign that brought Bush to the Vice Presidency in 1980, without the knowledge of then President Carter. (an allusion to the "October Surprise" allegations)

The opportunity was presented by the rumors of womanizing, which Hart accused unnamed candidates of spreading, and which well-timed accounts of his marital difficulties seemed to confirm. These rumors laid the foundation for the set-up, giving it a plausibility that might not be available if it had been launched out of thi air. Superficially it may seem that the idea of Gary Hart being "set up" is just another outrageous conspiracy theory. But before quickly dismissing this concept some investigation of political dirty tricks deeply woven into the fabric of America history must be explored.

The history of political dirty tricks within the intelligence community is long and noteworthy. The very first such covert operation was the subversion of the 1948 Italian elections. From there elections in France, Chile, Puerto Rico, the Phillipines, and South Vietnam were all victims of electoral dirty tricks.

If the CIA was indeed directly involved in the Gary Hart set-up there would have had to have been a willingness to violate its own charter, a charter which forbade a domestic role for the agency. In later chapters we will attempt to demonstrate that the agency violated its' charter almost as frequently as it upheld it…
agents trained in these techniques ever went to work for political campaigns within the United States. Linebarger was said to have hoped aloud that this would never occur, because if it did the American democratic system would be destroyed.

…. Former (CIA) agent Joseph Smith makes note of CIA psychological warfare expert Paul Linebarger's misgivings about the agency in Smith's book *Portrait of a Cold Warrior – Second Thoughts of a Top CIA Agent.*

Smith says that Linebarger clearly loved the thinking and inventiveness required by psychological warfare and 'black propaganda' operations, but feared the worst if 'Black propaganda' operations are operations in which the entity that motivates a news story is disguised in such a way that it appears it is actually a legitimate source, e.g. the media, who is generating the story. The black propaganda operator, however, is in fact the hidden source – in many cases a member of the intelligence community. The CIA's covert ops policy provides many instances in which black propaganda can be, and has been, used. And to circulate any black propaganda necessary to cover its clandestine operations, the CIA has at its disposal the most efficient of all dissemination vehicles – the propaganda asset – a plant within the media.

CHAPTER TWO: PROPAGANDA ASSETS

When CIA director William Colby admitted that the CIA controlled 40 journalists in the early 70s, it was against the backdrop of the National Student Association scandal. It was revealed that the CIA had been funding the NSA to the tune of $150,000 a year for 20 years. (Colby's revelation) …was for the most part ignored by the same media that the agency sought to compromise.

The number forty was certainly too low an estimation and might well have represented a combination of disinformation and the sort of "foot in the door" approach that the CIA had used to extract leverage from Congressional committees whose role it was to oversee intelligence organizations.

When the CIA admitted that it had infiltrated the media in a small way, unless there was an abundance of public opposition, the agency put the oversight committees on notice that it intended to proceed with its use of journalist/agents in place. If there had been a great hue and cry, those 40 "propaganda assets" might well have been sacrificed, leaving many more journalist/agents in place.

It might even have served the agency's purpose to get rid of some of the more ineffective or suspicious agents and demonstrate the sort of responsiveness on the part of the agency that could be trade for political capital. In any event, it was a win-win situation for the agency. Colby's remarks might even have been interpreted as a trial balloon.

As early as the 1950s, Joseph Smith, an agent stationed variously in Singapore, the Philippines and Indonesia, recalls using over two dozen journalist/agents himself in the Philippines alone, that the agency more or less owned an entire newspaper in Indonesia, and was able to plant disinformation on a wire service in Singapore (including one false story that helped set the stage for US intervention in Indochina). It seems unlikely that just a three nation area on the periphery of southeast Asia accounted for almost all of the CIA's journalist/agents.

Since very little was made of the frightening situation of a government agency quietly seeking control of the "guardian of liberty," the free press (a situation unanticipated by the authors of the Constitution) it was now safe for the agency to move to seek virtual control of the mass media, at least at the national level. Since CIA agents within the media might well be able to cooperate with one another and advance one another's careers, the journalist who did not hold CIA approved views might find themselves increasingly blocked when it came to advancement and out of the all-important information loop so vital to a journalist. And since the journalist/agent would have much greater access to the information available to the agency, their career could be on a relative fast track when compared to their peers.

We asked former CBS and CNN correspondent Daniel Schorr about his opinions concerning CIA infiltration of the media. Schorr, considered one of the deans of American journalism, had had a long and often controversial career.

He had worked with Edward R. Murrow and Walter Cronkite, had been an almost confidant of Nikita Krushchev before Schorr's arrest and removal from the Soviet Union, and had nearly been held in contempt of Congress. Schorr had departed in stormy and dramatic fashion from both CBS and CNN. He had been the CBS Watergate correspondent and had won three Emmys for that coverage. Currently he works for National Public Radio (NPR).

During an introduction by fellow journalist Bill Hosakawa for a talk that Schorr would be giving entitled "Confessions of a Journalist at 75," (also the subject of a book Schorr had just written), Schorr revealed that he had also had a career in Army Intelligence. Even with this knowledge it was difficult for the authors to envision that a journalist with Schorr's reputation for courage and feistiness could be compromised.

Schorr had recently jumped on the anti-Oliver Stone bandwagon over Stone's movie *JFK*, referring to Stone's work as an "assault on history." Schorr remains part of a shrinking minority in insisting that Lee Harvey Oswald acted alone and that the CIA and FBI destruction of files relating to Oswald were due to "bureaucratic embarrassment."

In the case of the CIA this "embarrassment" was the agency's alleged worry that Oswald had acted on a Fidel Castro speech that had been carried in the newspapers threatening retaliation because of the assassination attempts on Castro. Schorr's theory is that if the Warren

Commission had had access to the CIA files, it would have found out about the CIA-Mafia plots to assassinate Castro. ….When asked about CIA infiltration in the media, Schorr noted that William Paley, chairman of CBS had agreed to "provide cover" for CIA agents as journalists during Schorr's tenure "at the height of the Cold War." Schorr noted two specific examples of this – the network's providing cover to agents at the CBS bureaus in Egypt and Sweden….Schorr went on to say that there may have been others, but that after Church hearings the CIA promised not to use journalists as agents in the future.

The Senate's Church Committee (of which Gary Hart was one of the most vociferous members) along with the House's Pike Committee and the blue ribbon Rockefeller Commission were all formed to explore allegations of illegal activities undertaken by the CIA in the 1950s and 1960s, including but not limited to, illegal domestic surveillance of anti-war activists, mail opening, drug experiments on unsuspecting persons and, of course, assassination attempts undertaken against foreign leaders. It is difficult to believe the Schorr would really accept at face value that the CIA promises to the Church committee was the end of journalist/agents.

His background in Army Intelligence would likely tell him that that the agency was employing a favorite tactic for surviving hostile interrogation. That is to appear be fully cooperative by releasing information that the interrogators did not know, but which is not vital or has become irrelevant, so that critical operations and secrets are protected.

William Colby, director of the CIA at the time of the Church hearings put it this way: "I didn't rush to volunteer anything. It had to be dragged out of me; there was no other choice. I was teased at the time about going to confession. But no, I came to a very deliberate decision. We were under attack. I had to be responsive to the committees on the larger question in order <u>to protect the real secrets."</u>

Colby went on to say, "…you wish it did not have to come out, but if it does the damage isn't that great. I took the position strongly that we should protect the secrets, the people and some of the technology, and we should try not to stonewall on anything else." So much for the belief that the Church committee exposed all CIA wrongdoing and/or assurances that they would not happen again in the future.

…Schorr once inspired journalists as well as cognizant citizens everywhere by stating that he would rather go to jail than reveal the source who had given him highly confidential congressional documents relating to the investigation of intelligence agencies. It is likely that few considered that Schorr would have been in far more danger if he revealed the source, if indeed the source was a contact in the intelligence community, or that Schorr knew he would not go to jail – i.e. the fix was in.

…Schorr neither surrendered the name of his source, nor spent any time in jail. At the last minute Congress blinked and did not issue a Contempt of Congress citation. Likewise, Schorr's arrest and expulsion from the Soviet Union might not have been "trumped up" charges claimed by Schorr friend Bill Hosakawa. Whatever the case, Schorr's statement that journalism is the perfect cover for an intelligence agent may well be more revealing that Schorr had intended.

A recent book, *Silent Coup*, has alleged that the fast track of Bob Woodward at the *Washington Post* is just such a phenomenon. It cites Woodward's early intelligence training and alleges that Woodward invented his "Deep Throat" source to explain his extensive inside knowledge. Certainly, the presence of an agent as apparently credible, influential and powerful as Woodward would give the agency opportunities for propaganda and disinformation that no government press ever could.

How many respected publishers and esteemed journalists are in the CIA's pocket? The real answer to that question may well explain why the American media appears to speak with a single voice so often. It may well explain the so-called media "feeding frenzy" that descended on the Hart campaign in 1987 as well as the anti-Stone phenomenon.

Never known to leave any of its bases uncovered, however, the CIA not only seeks to infiltrate the media, but publishes its own materials as well. In 1967, Praeger Publications admitted to publishing at least 15 books on behalf of the agency. Doubleday published a book entitled *The Penkovsky Papers* whose publication was solely aimed at giving disinformation to the Soviets.

UPDATE: Conversely, as confirmed by the author's own experience refusal to cooperate with spiking a story that has been ordered spiked either by consensus or government interests will seriously harm a journalistic career. The author had been offered the vacation desk for the local headquarters of one of the international wire services. At the time, the NBC station in Oklahoma City had reported on the possible identity of what was called "John Doe 2" in the Oklahoma City bombing, an individual who also might have been an Iraqi intelligence agent. Unfortunately I shared my feeling that the story needed further investigation with the wire service. I was told to forget it, there wasn't anything to it. When I explained some of the reasons I believed the situation deserved further investigation, I was not given the vacation desk in Denver.

This is not to say that not having "flexible" journalistic ethics is harmful to one's career only when dealing with large "plugged in" media. There is a reason that for the most part, my journalistic career has been freelance. I was on the staff of a small newspaper in a small Colorado mountain town when I was told to spike a story I had been working on about a company who intended to use a uranium mining method that would have widely polluted the area's ground water. I was shortly after fired.

The company, Wyoming Minerals, intended to pump chemicals that dissolved uranium into the aquifers in the area and then pump the dissolved uranium and groundwater to the surface, retrieving the uranium and pumping the groundwater back into the ground. They claimed that their mining method presented no danger to the area's groundwater. Unfortunately for their state licenses, at least, an investigative piece in the *Rocky Mountain News* reported that where this had been done in Texas, state authorities had fined Wyoming Minerals when contaminated groundwater had been detected.

(That is not to say that I am against all mining. Mining is essential to modern life. I have held mining claims and conducted mining operations in the past and was made a mining engineer in 1983.)

Most of the time propaganda assets or intelligence agents operating without cover, prefer to approach journalists who might not be playing ball in a friendly manner and impart the agency's talking points, which may or may not contain disinformation.

In 2000 I wrote a freelance article for *The Washington Free Press* entitled "Genetic Bullets." Although I won part of a 2001 Project Censored award for the article (Project Censored is administered by Sonoma State University and designed to award and bring attention to important under-reported or spiked stories), it was a relatively easy issue to investigate. It was also very dangerous if you got too close to it as evidenced by the death of Danny Casolaro and the imprisonment of his source and who now is far too paranoid to expand on what he told Casolaro.

"Genetic Bullets" revealed not only that the governments of some nations had commissioned research into the creation of "ethnically specific biological weapons," but that the Human Genome project was actually doing some of the basic research that would be necessary to create such weapons. Links to the article and to Project Censored are in the links section at the end of the book.

Interestingly, the Human Genome project's research proved the idea of separate "races," within the human race, were scientifically invalid. Does it not become much more difficult to concoct a weapon that would eliminate an entire ethnicity without eliminating the entire human race? Difficult, but not impossible.

A short time after the article came out I was in downtown Seattle with some Canadian journalists and friends when we "ran into" a man who identified himself as involved with a branch of military intelligence. He made a point of telling me that just because the government was engaged in research did not mean that they were going to use it. Further, he contended, that a lot of the time if we think some other country is doing a certain type of research, even if that research is abhorrent, we are forced to engage in it as well. Consider the Manhattan Project. We have to have a contingency plan for any scenario.

One of my Canadian friends in a sort of semi-snarky manner asked him if that meant the US had a contingency plan for invading Canada.

44

"Of course," he answered, "you wouldn't want to feel left out would you?"

Everybody had a good laugh (although it seemed as though one or two of the Canadians had a very polite but still nervous laugh) and we went on our separate ways. Despite that encounter being friendly, I was not so sure that that would be the end of it, and have not relaxed any of my normal security precautions. The most important security precaution of an investigative reporter is to report all he knows as soon as he knows it in the hopes that those who might wish to squelch the story realize that if the reporter were to come to harm it would do a great deal to confirm the accuracy of his report. In that event the powers whose ox is gored by the report will instead do their best to discredit the reporter instead.

How he knew who I was or if it was just a bizarre coincidence, I am still uncertain.

CHAPTER THREE – DOMESTIC COVERT ACTIVITIES AND MIND CONTROL

...the very first acknowledged covert action undertaken by the CIA after the passage of the National Security Act was the rigging of the Italian elections in 1948. J. Edgar Hoover, director of the FBI, was an outspoken opponent of the act, warning that it would create an "American Gestapo." Worried about a Communist victory in these elections the CIA sought to covertly support the other parties in the election.

These early CIA officials worried that there might be no legal basis (under U.S. law – there was obviously none under Italian laws) for covert activities of this sort in the authorizing legislation that created the agency. Lawrence Houston, the CIA's first general counsel, informed the directors that he could not find any specific authorization for covert activities in the National Security Act, but that if the Agency was authorized by the Congress the agency could then proceed.

The early concern with adhering to the letter of the National Security Act would soon be a casualty of the Cold War.

In 1962 and 1964 as leftist Salvador Allende sought election in Chile, the CIA provided at least $4 million to Allende's middle of the road and right wing opponents. These funds included not only direct funds to the political parties but an overall propaganda campaign including planted newspaper stories.

It is estimated that in 1964 the CIA footed over half the bill for Allende's opposition. In 1970, the year Allende would beat the odds, then director Richard Helms was told that over $10 million was available to defeat Allende and more would be forthcoming if necessary. At the time America was still very much involved in Vietnam....Very similar activities occurred in the Philippines and Indonesia in the 1950s and in Puerto Rico during every election where independence for the island was considered. No nation was considered above agency manipulation, perhaps not even the United States itself.

....Indeed covert operations during Presidential elections seem to have been the rule rather than the exception in recent elections. Most Republican partisans are well aware of the allegations that voter fraud in Chicago may have won John Kennedy the White House in 1960.

Assassination marred the 1964 and 1968 campaigns. In 1980 the Congressional Albosta report contended that pro-Reagan intelligence operatives within the Carter White House fed vital campaign information, perhaps even Carter's debate briefing papers to the Reagan campaign. !988 was thought to be an exception, the year of the negative ad and Willie Horton, but were Democrats steered towards a weak candidate by sophisticated and well-orchestrated behind the scenes maneuvers.

Allegedly there is also further precedent for media involvement in aid of CIA dirty tricks. According to former CIA executive and author Victor Marchetti, the CIA ran an "operation" against the House Assassinations Committee which had been set up to investigate the

47

assassinations of JFK and Martin Luther King, Jr. Indeed a CIA employee was caught breaking into the committee's safe. Whether by design or accident, members of the media aided attempts to discredit the committee even before any serious investigation had started.

David Burnham of the *New York Times* and George Lardner, Jr., of the *Washington Post*, nearly brought the committee down by printing attacks on the committee's Chief Counsel. Interestingly, Burnham was with David Ferrie, Lee Harvey Oswald's Civil Air Patrol commander as well as a possible CIA and mob contractor, on the night that Ferrie died. Karen Silkwood, the Kerr-McGee nuclear plant whistle blower, was also with Burnham on the night of her mysterious death.

Chief Counsel Sprague forced Rep. Henry Gonzales, a Congressman who had witnessed the Kennedy assassination off of the committee and then was forced to quit himself. Gonzales claimed that the investigation was being sabotaged "because vast and powerful forces, including the country's most sophisticated element won't stand for it."

He further said that the committee was a "put up job and hideous farce that was never intended to work," concluding that "there's something very strange going on in this country --- strange and frightening."
One area of CIA research and experimentation is particularly frightening. This is the area of mind control...Although the research has disappeared from public view it is unlikely that the agency has completely abandoned the effort.

Allegedly the agency began its mind control research after viewing the "confessions" of Cardinal Mindzenty in 1949 in which it was apparent, at least to the agency, that some sort of Soviet mind control must have been at work. The agency argued that if the Soviets had some sort of mind control capability that we must be able to match it, and the first of a series of mind control programs was born.

…Ironically one of the first "guinea pigs" of early mind control experiments was a member of the Luciano syndicate that first brought the forces of organized crime and American intelligence together in the Second World War. August Del Gracio was given cigarettes that contained marijuana in an early attempt to find a so-called truth drug by the Office of Strategic Services (OSS). He was then questioned about mob activities and apparently was felt to have answered truthfully and comprehensively.

The first CIA program was called Project Bluebird. Project Bluebird's initial mission may have been to root out double agents and communist moles who had attempted to or successfully managed to infiltrate the agency. It was later merged with or supplanted by Project Artichoke whose goal was essentially to create a "human robot," an agent or contact who would obey the most unpleasant order unthinkingly.

Interestingly the widow of Russian exile Count George DeMohrenschildt, a friend of Marina and Lee Harvey Oswald as well as a possible CIA agent, believed that he had been programmed to take his life on command.

She claimed DeMohrenschildt was drugged surreptitiously. Dr. Charles Mendoza, his alleged doctor, provided a false forwarding address after treating him and apparently gave him unidentified injections.

DeMohrenschildt allegedly committed suicide on the day the House Assassinations Committee located him after he "received a phone call."

...One of the expendable secrets that CIA director Colby gave to the Church Committee was that unwitting Americans were secretly filmed to test the effects of drugs given to them by CIA employed prostitutes. This may be significant for a number of reasons, not the least of which being that it demonstrated the willingness of the CIA to employ ladies of the evening in intelligence work. That theme is found here later and may well have been at least partially instrumental in answering the question of what happened to Gary Hart.

UPDATE FROM OBJECTIVE EVIL: SATANIC CULTS IN US INTELLIGENCE

The most illuminating and readily available published literature by Aquino on the subject of psychological warfare is entitled *From Psyop to Mindwar: The Psychology of Victory*, which Aquino, then a major, co-wrote with Colonel Paul E. Vallely.

Although the paper was briefly alluded to in Jonathan Vankin's *Conspiracies, Cover-ups and Crimes,* its true significance cannot be understood without some knowledge of the more or less secret projects that the paper outlines with a broad brush. It becomes clear early in the paper that the line between psychological warfare operations and mind control is unclear or else being deliberately obfuscated. In spite of the media rubber-stamped disinformation that the government is out of the mind control business following the Congressional revelations of the 70s, the paper states that the government has not only continued its research but has achieved some measure of success.

"Psychotronic research is in its infancy," the paper states, "but the US Army already possesses an operational weapons system designed to do what LTC Alexander would like ESP to do – except that this weapons system uses existing communications media. It seeks to map the minds of neutral and enemy individuals and then change them in accordance with US national interests. It does this on a wide scale, embracing military units, regions, nations and blocs. In its present form it is called Psychological Operations (PSYOP)."

…A June 1992 Army symposium acknowledged the Army's possession of these sorts of weapons including a directed energy low frequency sound weapons system capable of producing psychological disorientation as well as physical incapacitation.

A January 4, 1993 *Wall Street Journal* article added that infrasound weapons could also be fine tuned to produce nausea, vomiting or bowel spasms and added that the Justice Department was busily researching whether the system could be used in civil disturbances…

…Scientists discovered that the human mind could be accessed at frequencies of 425-450 MHz, an idea that would fit both with "Mindwar" and the book, *The Cycles of Heaven* which was cited in "Mindwar."…The Senate hearings held by Frank Church in the mid-1970s disclosed that the joint Army-CIA mind control project, MKULTRA, consisted of over 180 subprojects. One called MKUltra subproject 142 sought to control the brain through the use of electrical stimulation, using a remote control system to control the brain of the subject from great distances. There have been other agency funded research facilities with mind control potentials, but innocent sounding names, such as the UCLA Behavior Modification Institute. Until "Mindwar," however, no non-secret government document ever reported that the government had an operational mind control system capable of mass behavioral modification, the most palatable euphemism for mind control.

…If the reader is not entirely clear that there are no spectators to "Mindwar," the authors make it crystal clear. "Mindwar must target all participants if it is to be effective. It must not only weaken the enemy, it must strengthen the United States. It strengthens the United States by denying enemy propaganda access to our people, and by explaining and emphasizing to our people the rationale for our national interest in a specific war."

52

CHAPTER FOUR: A STARTLING SERIES OF COINCIDENCES

On September 18, 1991, in response to our earlier call to the *Miami Herald* when we spoke to Susan Rodin (assistant to Doug Clifton, executive editor of the *Herald* as well as one of the reporters who confronted Hart outside of his Washington D.C. townhouse), we received a letter from Tom Fiedler, the paper's political editor and the reporter who allegedly received the anonymous tip that set the *Herald* surveillance in motion.

Curiously the letter stated that Heath Merriweather, former *Herald* executive editor (who at press time held the same position at the *Detroit Free Press*) passed along our request for an account of the *Herald's* actions and thinking during the Hart affair. (We had not been able to contact Mr. Merriweather. Interestingly, when we spoke to Susan Rodin, she stated that we should contact Mr. Merriweather and neglected to mention Mr. Clifton's important role in this affair.) Fiedler's letter comprised a 16 page account of the newspaper's activities and surveillance involving the Hart-Rice affair, which Fiedler made clear was the *Herald's* unbending final position on the matter.

Unfortunately for our understanding of the affair, the *Herald's* account seemed to present information that was either directly contradicted by revelations made by the *Herald* soon after the Hart debacle was revealed or that seemed to present more questions than it answered. The reaction of the *Herald* reporters in either instance appeared to show an odd lack of professional curiosity, objectivity and thoroughness.

On May 4, 1987, the day that the *Herald's* story made front page news all over the nation, Jim Savage, the *Herald's* investigative editor was quoted as saying that reporter Jim McGee received the anonymous tip that started the investigation of Hart. In the "official" *Herald* account, however, it was Fiedler that received the tip. According to the account, the tipster, a woman called, apparently hoping to sell pictures of Hart and her "friend," who was allegedly having an affair with the Senator.

Most of the speculation as to the source of the tip has centered on Lynn Armandt, Rice's model friend, who was the source of the *People* article on the affair, a history of the affair that left many questions unanswered. Armandt, incidentally, has sued the authors and publishers of *Blue Thunder*, who not only allege that she was the source of the tip to the *Herald,* but who also assert that she behaved as a "madam," (presumably to Rice's "hooker") during the affair.

Armandt's legal action could be seen as either one of genuine outrage or a sinister attempt to scare off speculation about the Hart matter before it begins. In any event, if Armandt is not the source of the tip, then the real identity of the source of the tip becomes even more significant. Clearly Armandt as the source of the tip was the most consistent with the "face value" scenario of the affair. That scenario is, for lack of a better term, that Armandt apparently "sold out" her friend, Rice, for momentary fame and fortune.

According to *Blue Thunder*, Rice and Armandt have apparently been seen together on quite friendly terms (following the scandal). If Rice was indeed as indignant about Armandt's actions as she indicated to Barbara Walters, Rice is apparently a very forgiving person and put the matter behind her rather quickly.

According to Fiedler, he initially rebuffed the tipster, telling her to consider the charges she was making and call back at another time if she wanted to pursue the matter further. When she called back again Fiedler said that he felt it was a "crank call." Rather than hang up on this "crank call," however, Fiedler stayed on the phone with the caller for 90 minutes. According to the caller, Hart had met "her friend" (Rice) at a party on board a yacht some weeks earlier.

Rice had allegedly given Hart her phone number at that time. The caller went on to say that Hart then later called Rice and asked her to accompany him on a cruise where they stayed overnight (no doubt the "Monkey Business" cruise to Bimini), although at the time the caller said that she did not know where Hart and Rice went on the cruise. The caller again asked the *Herald* about their interest in purchasing the pictures, clearly indicating that the caller had mercenary motives, but when the *Herald* declined the offer the tipster apparently decided to part with the information she possessed for free, and she had a great deal of information.

The caller went on to say she knew Hart had called Rice on a number of occasions while on the campaign trail; curiously, she also knew the places (from which) the calls had originated as well as the dates that the calls had been made. She alleged that there were at least three calls like this made from Kansas, Alabama and Georgia. Apparently the called had gone to a great deal of trouble to be quite thorough in this regard.

The caller had initially indicated that she was a "liberal Democrat," (people were not in the habit of using the word 'liberal" by itself to describe themselves – at that point in American history, the term had fallen out of favor and become a 'dirty word'), so the caller appeared to have no political axe to grind. Why then had she bothered to make careful note of the dates and places that Hart allegedly made the calls to Rice?

The comprehensive nature of the tipster's information would seem to indicate either the cooperation of the phone company or the cooperation of Rice, who, while being exact to the most minute detail about Hart's calls to her, was nonetheless not forthcoming at all about the destination of her cruise with Hart. Apparently the *Herald* was not interested in or willing to investigate these apparent contradictions.

The caller still had not named Donna Rice. Why Rice was not implicated by the caller is not entirely clear. She had been as specific as possible on every other detail.

Apparently during a later call, the tipster, who apparently was privy to Rice's itinerary, told the *Herald* that Rice was planning to spend the weekend with Hart at his townhouse in Washington D.C. They would be meeting on Friday night, she said.

Immediately after the scandal hit the newspapers, Savage referred to the information given by the tipster on Rice, her flight, and the Washington weekend as "vague." However, because the tipster had accurately known the dates that Hart was in Miami as well as the dates that he was in various other states along the campaign trail, the *Herald* decided to go all out in investigating this "vague" information.

Curiously, Fiedler himself states "….it remained conceivable that a campaign dirty trickster could have gotten Hart's schedule and elaborately fabricated the story." Yet beyond conceding this obvious possibility, the *Herald* put its doubts aside and never investigated even after the Hart campaign was reduced to the status of one of history's most famous disasters.

According to the May 4, 1987 *Denver Post*, the *Miami Herald* originally claimed the tip was given to Jim McGee. Jim Savage, investigative editor of the *Herald* was the source of the account of the reporter's actions. This account included (based on what was said to be "vague" information) that a woman and Hart were to meet on the weekend McGee boarded a flight to Washington.

McGee noticed a woman on the flight who allegedly fit the description of the woman that Hart was to meeting.

57

As imprecise as this information was, it proved to be amazingly exact – the woman on the plane was, in fact, Rice.

What is so outstanding about Rice that allows a reporter to be able to identify her from a large group of passengers based on "vague" information? Was it just coincidental that McGee would be taking the exact same flight as Rice? And why, after supposedly identifying Rice, did McGee not follow her, but instead drive immediately to Hart's townhouse. Perhaps McGee had inside knowledge of the fact that Rice would not be meeting Hart in an expensive hotel (which would seem like a reasonable expectation for the locale of a discreet rendezvous), but instead at Hart's townhouse. Considering the circumstances, the events of that evening are not clear and in fact very puzzling, unless things had somehow been scripted.

Although the tipster had not given the *Herald* either Rice's name or the exact flight information, she had given a very general description of the woman Hart was to meet as being a part-time actress, blonde, in her late 20s and with a "rich Southern drawl." From that description, and from the information that Hart and Rice were to meet on Friday night, *Herald* reporter McGee whisked off to the airport. In an almost unbelievable coincidence McGee managed to spot Rice getting onto her flight and take that same flight with her, despite the fact that there were five flights between Washington and Miami that evening.

Additionally, there is nothing in the *Herald* account that suggests that could not even be sure Rice had not already arrived in Washington earlier that day or even earlier in the week.

Anyone who has ever attempted to make connections with someone they have never met, even when the flight of that individual is known, would have trouble believing the coincidence of McGee's anecdote. Yet for some reason, being able to later state that the woman on the plane and Rice were one and the same was important to the *Herald* reporters. Perhaps they felt that this substantiated the story.

McGee followed Rice onto the plane and watched as Rice and an unidentified companion, also a blonde, took their seats. During the flight the two women seemed to know each other quite well, yet this other woman was apparently never identified. Upon landing, Rice was greeted in the baggage claim area by another woman, this time a brunette, also unidentified. It was at this point that McGee broke off the tail on Rice, feeling that he might be following the wrong individual. When this later proved not to be the case, the question of who these other women were and what information they might have had also apparently never occurred to the *Herald*.

Meanwhile, Fiedler claimed that the *Herald* was unaware of the location of Hart's Washington D.C. townhouse. Again coincidence intervened and the press secretary to Senator Bob Graham, who was calling the *Herald* on an "unrelated" matter, volunteered the location, apparently unconcerned that the home address of the man most likely to be the next President might be a dangerous piece of information to be giving out indiscriminately.

At 9:30 that evening McGee and then Knight Ridder news editor Doug Clifton saw Hart and "the very same woman he (McGee) had seen on the airplane," coming out of Hart's townhouse together. Certainly questions arise as to why a news editor was sent to stake out the Senator's townhouse based on unclear information.

McGee, upon allegedly seeing Rice leave the townhouse, claimed he was "stunned" that she was the same blonde he had been following on the airplane. Now the reason McGee needed to see Rice on the airplane became clear; in seeing Rice twice, prima facie evidence was constituted for the *Herald*.

McGee immediately ran to telephone his superiors in Miami and request additional reporters and a photographer. According to the *Herald* account the time was 9:33, just three minutes after McGee claimed to have seen Hart and Rice emerge from Hart's townhouse. As he was on the phone McGee supposedly again saw Hart and Rice getting out of Hart's car and returning to Hart's townhouse. The purpose of Hart's three minute ride with Rice was never discussed, although the *Herald* account notes that "the series of coincidences that drove the story continued."

Later that evening the rest of the *Herald* team arrived. Perhaps in an effort to in some way justify the surveillance, Fiedler circled the famous "follow me around" quote in the Sunday *New York Times,* which was in Fiedler's possession, despite the fact that it was early Saturday and the article had not yet hit the newsstands. (note: Hart states that he never made such a comment.)

To their credit the *Herald* acknowledged that their surveillance was far from airtight; however, why the *Herald* was not concerned that their coverage might therefore unfairly assail the character of Hart is never explained. When the *Herald* confronted that he was being set up, there was never any inkling that the paper would not go with the story, despite some scrambling by members of the Hart campaign.

William Broadhurst, who had been identified variously as Hart's lawyer, fundraiser and merely a Hart supporter, attempted to offer the *Herald* interview with Rice and her friend and fellow Monkey Business passenger, Lynn Armandt, in exchange for holding off on the publication of the story for 24 hours. In a prosecutorial tone, Fiedler declined the offer, stating that he felt the deal came "with a huge escape clause."

Of course, the *Herald* did publish the story. The Hart campaign responded that Donna Rice had left by way of the parking garage minutes after arriving at Hart's townhouse and had returned because she had "left something behind," only to leave again shortly thereafter. (It would follow that this is the reason for the three minute ride in which McGee followed Rice and Hart.) The *Herald* admitted that such a scenario was a possibility, but they did not believe it.

The first publication of the story by the *New York Times* was relegated to page 12 and emphasized the dispute between the Hart campaign and the *Herald.* Clearly major, but certainly not fatal damage had been done to the Hart campaign. That changed, however, when Donna Rice emerged and the damage rapidly worsened.

And what about Donna Rice? 1988 was also the "year of the bimbo." Fawn Hall, Jessica Hahn and Rice were all labeled "bimbos" by the media, each scandalously linked to a high profile male figure and each, to some degree, using that situation for own gain. Jessica Hahn, who claimed PTL evangelist Jim Baker raped her, truly capitalized on her notoriety. She posed nude for *Playboy,* agreed to several public interviews and even acquired a 900-number on which someone eager to part with their money could call and find out the latest goings on in Hahn's fascinating life. Hahn seemed to take every show-biz offer that came her way, from hosting mud wrestling to talk radio.

But were the others not "bimbos" after all, but seductive women deeply involved in the inner workings of the government and its agencies? Why did Hall and Rice both need a publicist (a publicist whom they shared) and yet for the most part refuse to capitalize on their notoriety? Hall, the paper shredding secretary to the Iran-Contra affair's Oliver North, has not appeared in print for quite some time and is quietly pursuing a legitimate career in broadcasting.

Rice refused offers to pose nude, despite the fact that she had earlier posed semi-topless, and except for a brief commercial career with a jeans company, she has refused all offers of fame and fortune and is reportedly living unpretentiously with a family in northern Virginia and "working with children."

Was Rice in fact a very moral and idealistic individual who was able to resist cashing in on her infamy? If so, this would seem to make the Hart-Rice affair even more tragic. Or was Rice's aversion to the limelight merely at the urging of a well-schooled spook? At the time of the Hart affair, Rice apparently was unconcerned with being photographed on the Senator's lap. In light of her behavior at the time of the affair, her current avoidance of media attention becomes all the more puzzling.

Amazingly, Rice was not at all shy the day following the *Herald* story, when reports of possible flaws in the *Herald's* surveillance might have caused the Hart story to become non-news. Rice was not timid when she went public, and while denying a sexual liaison with the Senator, dropped the Monkey Business bombshell, giving the story new life.

What made the *Herald's* revelations all the more damaging was that Rice had given the appearance of attempting to help Hart. The articles profiling Rice, which immediately appeared all over the nation after she was named, described her as being a very bright individual. If so, it is interesting that in attempting to help Hart she would add another nail to the coffin.

The articles profiling Rice were interesting also when viewed with some healthy skepticism. First, the amount of information available about Rice on the same she emerged as the "other woman" in the Hart affair was surprising, and quite puzzling. One article described her as a "young Christian" who dated a Southern Baptist minister and attended Billy Graham crusades. At the same time it was pointed out that she posed semi-topless for a promotional poster for a Miami area bar. Another article described her as a "jet-setter" and quoted the maintenance man at her high rise apartment as saying she was always "flying off" somewhere. At the same time she was described as a part-time model and actress, her apparent full time work being a pharmaceutical company salesperson for the south Florida area.

Those jobs hardly seemed to fit as the daytime professions of a "jet setter," as those folks are usually thought of as the idle rich, not local salespeople aspiring to an acting and modeling career in their spare time.

Her circle of friends and acquaintances, however, was certainly jet-set. In addition to the Eagle's Don Henley, who hosted the Aspen New Year's party where Rice first encountered Hart, Rice had apparently been romantically involved with Prince Albert of Monaco, was a friend of Frank Sinatra Jr.. and numerous other celebrities, the most interesting of whom was billionaire arms dealer and alleged "intelligence asset" of a number of services Adnan Khashoggi.

If Rice was indeed always flying off somewhere she would hardly have been an effective local salesperson for a drug company and the small time modeling and acting work she had received in the past would not seem sufficient to pay the bills for a jet setting life. It seems likely that someone else had to be paying Rice's bills.

The articles also mentioned that Rice ran into Hart again at a political fundraising party on board a yacht in Florida on March 1, 1988, a full two months and nearly 2000 miles from their first meeting in Aspen on New Year's eve. No one has made a great deal of that coincidence or of the fact that, according to another background article, Rice "had absolutely no interest in politics."

The day following the Rice articles, when a Bahamian Customs official suggested that Hart was lying about being unable to leave Bimini overnight, Hart received and scandalous headlines in almost every major newspaper in the country for three consecutive days, which was more than any candidate, even a candidate with a large lead in the polls, could survive. The whole affair began to take on the appearance of a well orchestrated media lynching.

UPDATE 1: FROM *ALL THE TRUTH IS OUT*
WAS DONNA RICE A "HONEY POT" AGENT?
Two of the most plausible sounding conspiracy theories involving the Hart affair involve deliberate actions taken by either William Broadhurst as a bribed fixer, Lynn Armandt pulling the strings and/or Donna Rice as a "honey pot" agent.

If Rice is to be believed, however, there was no honey for Hart. From *All The Truth is Out* although Rice, more even than Hart currently refuses to publicly discuss her role in the role, she has discussed the affair privately:

65

"Once over drinks, one of Hart's close aides from the period told me that Rice, like Hart, had steadfastly denied, even in private, having consummated an affair. I asked him whether he was actually suggesting that Hart, despite his reputation for promiscuity at the time, hadn't slept with the woman who would forever be linked to his ruined ambitions. The former aide looked around the bar and leaned closer to me, his voice dropping to a whisper. 'I fear not,' he said, looking genuinely pained."

UPDATE #2: WAS THE IDENTITY OF THE *MIAMI HERALD* INFORMANT REVEALED BY *THE NEW YORK TIMES* IN 2014?

In a September 22, 2014 *Miami Herald* article unflatteringly entitled "Who blabbed about Gary Hart-Donna Rice affair" reporter Greg Garvin reports that the *New York Times* "....has named a South Florida woman it says was the source of a *Miami Herald* story 27 years ago that wrecked the candidacy of Democrat Gary Hart," and it's not Lynn Armandt.
Of course, only *Herald* itself and the informant would be able to absolutely confirm the identity of the tipster.
Garvin explains "The *Herald's* report was triggered by an anonymous source who had seen the married Hart partying with Rice...(but) The *Herald* has never identified her."
Nor did the *Herald* take issue with the *Times* story.
"In an account published in the Sunday *New York Times magazine*...(the tipster is identified as)...Dana Weems, a Broward County clothing designer. Weems...confirmed she's the woman in the *Times* story but wouldn't discuss it further.

This is not the first time Weem's name has come up in connection with the scandal. In 1987, the *Atlanta Constitution* reported that Rice believed she was the tipster. Weems flatly denied it: 'No, I did not call the *Miami Herald*."

CHAPTER FIVE: THE POST'S MYSTERIOUS ROLE

Perhaps one of the most curious circumstances of the entire affair involves the behavior of the *Washington Post.* Although the stories in the *Miami Herald* badly weakened the Hart campaign, even the *Herald* itself acknowledges that the last nail in the coffin was driven in by the *Washington Post.* Kevin Sweeney, at the time Hart's press secretary, also confirmed that the final decision by Hart to exit the 1988 campaign was made after Sweeney told Hart about a private detective's report commissioned by the *Post* but never released.

The detective's report obtained by the *Post* contained photographs that allegedly showed Hart entering and leaving a Washington woman's house on December 20, 1986, a full five months before the Rice affair. This date was also at least four months prior to a *Newsweek* profile of Hart, which the *Herald* mentioned as being the beginning of the "womanizing accusations" the would haunt the Senator's short campaign.

Who hired the investigator and why is still unknown, as is the means in which the *Post* obtained the detective's report. The *Post's* executive editor, Ben Bradlee, would not comment, invoking an apparent agreement with the source, and stating, incredibly, that he felt there was no political motive behind the surveillance. Again, the media was amazingly uninquisitive about who might be behind this extraordinary surveillance of the probably next President of the United States, and they simply took Bradlee's statements at face value.

What the *Post* did after it received the report is clear, however. The *Post* let the Hart campaign know it had the detective's report and implied that it would release the information and further damage not only Hart's rapidly declining political future but his already tarnished reputation as well. With this action the *Post* obviously crossed the line from reporting the news to becoming part of it, with an apparent outcome of outright blackmail of a major political candidate.

In fact the *Post* never made the detective's report public, even after Hart re-entered the race, by then badly (irreparably) wounded. If the *Post* never intended to use the report, why then would Sweeney have reported that the existence of the report was the key to Hart's decision to withdraw from the race? In acquiring a major exclusive story that it never used the *Post* seemed to be defying all journalistic logic.

In an effort to get a comment from the *Post* and hopefully clear up some of the confusion involving the newspaper's role in the Hart affair, we wrote to Ben Bradlee, vice president and certainly the most well known spokesman for the *Post*.

We presented a list of questions to Bradlee that existed at the time of Hart's withdrawal from the race. The reports were from a *Denver Post* article in which Sweeney is said to have contended that the final decision to withdraw from the race was made by Hart after the campaign had been informed of the private detective's report, at that time in the possession of the *Washington Post*.

Bradlee was quoted in the article as saying that he had independently verified the accuracy of the detective's report. A number of questions quickly came to mind, and, while they were not asked in the heat of the '88 campaign, we hoped that Bradlee might wish to clear the air and set the record straight. Mr. Bradlee's responses to our questions follow. The reader will note that we have inserted comments after Bradlee's answers which were not included in his letter to us.

Q. Since Paul Taylor (a *Post* reporter) approached Kevin Sweeney with the information in the detective's report, was it the *Washington Post's* intention to tell Hart to withdraw from the race or the *Post* would release the report.

Bradlee: *I must say that I find the first one (question) a little naïve. To my certain knowledge the Washington Post has never had any intention of telling any politician to do anything, much less threaten them with something if they didn't. That is not a newspaper's role. So the answer to the first question is a resounding no.*

Q. When did the *Post* obtain the report?

Bradlee: …a couple of days before Taylor talked to Sweeney.

Q. How did the post independently confirm the veracity of the facts of the report? Did the *Post* participate in the surveillance on December 20?

Bradlee: *The Post independently confirmed only that a long time relationship had existed and still existed between the senator and the woman. The Post did not participate in any surveillance.*

(Our comment: How did the *Post* confirm the prior and present existence of this relationship without surveillance? The *Post knew a relationship existed, yet was unable to characterize the nature of the relationship or how that knowledge was obtained.)*

Q. Is it possible to release any more information about who the detective was, who commissioned the surveillance and why?

Bradlee: *The answer is no because I have no confirmed information on the subject.*

(Our comment: If the *Post* has no "confirmed" information on the subject, that would make the *Post's* actions even more unfathomable. Either the *Post* is avoiding the issue or it had presumed Hart guilty before being tried if it had no confirmed information.)

Q. How are you able to be sure that there were no political motivations behind the report and who commissioned it? Bradlee: I think the motivations behind the report were plain and not political. We are not going to say who commissioned it.

(Our comment: Previously Bradlee had said he had "no confirmed" information on the subject. Now it seemed as though he had information but wished to cover it up.)

Q. Why did the *Post* not publish the contents of the report either before the Rice affair, prior to or after Hart's initial withdrawal from the race, or after Hart's re-entry into the race as a very badly wounded candidate?

Bradlee: *Once Hart withdrew from the race we felt the contents of the report was his business.*

(Our comment: The answer appears to clearly contradict Bradlee's answer to the first question in that the *Post* would have considered publication of the report in the event that Hart was a candidate and a strong one at that.)

Q. If the *Post* never intended to use the report, what was the purpose of informing the Hart campaign and others of the existence of the report?

Bradlee: *The answer to (this) question...has to do with lying. It seems to me that the report was germane in determining whether Hart was telling the truth about his private life. If he was, that was the end of it. If he wasn't we felt that was something the public had a right to know.*

(Our comment: How does Bradlee's answer relate to this question? He talks of the public's right to know, but then the *Post* did not release the report, only hinting that they had it. Also since the *Post* did not publish the report, and therefore "that was the end of it," as Bradlee had said, then one could deduce that Hart had indeed been telling the truth about his private life.)

Was this the same *Washington Post*, the watchdog of the political system? Wasn't the *Post* the paper of Woodward and Bernstein and Watergate? Maybe the *Post* was also the voice of the professional intelligence community.

In October 1977 Stansfield Turner, the Carter Administration's CIA director, fired 820 CIA personnel. Shortly after the incident, called the "Halloween massacre," CIA factions formed that were opposed to the Carter administration. In early 1979 another 250 CIA employees put in for retirement. At that time the *Washington Post* said in an article that "American intelligence is dying," and put the onus on Stansfield Turner, Carter's CIA director.

The *Post's* unique relationship with the CIA may have started with Phil Graham, brother of Katherine Graham and co-owner of the *Post* until his suicide in 1963. In World War II Phil had been in Army intelligence and reportedly was a believer in "mediapolitics," which was that a newspaper should attempt to mobilize support for the policy of the government (especially given the Cold War).

Phil was a close friend of Richard Helms, who would later become director of the CIA and Desmond Fitzgerald, the CIA's far east operative. Among other accomplishments, Fitzgerald may well have been the principal CIA representative who set up the Nationalist Chinese in northern Burma in the opium trade in 1949. It is widely speculated that Phil Graham first learned that *Newsweek* was for sale from Richard Helms, who grandfather was on the *Newsweek* board.

Besides the questionable journalistic methods of the *Miami Herald*, the *Washington Post*, CBS and the media in general, the role of *Newsweek* in the affair also bears further scrutiny. The *Miami Herald* political editor has been quoted as stating that one of the most important considerations in going after Hart was his "history" of womanizing. Curiously, that history had only become an issue a mere two weeks prior to the Rice affair, when *Newsweek* made reference to "rumors" of Hart's infidelity.

At the time there was nothing concrete in the rumors (although, of course, the *Post* surveillance had already occurred), and, ironically Fiedler wrote a front page article for the *Herald* on the subject of the rumors that he later characterized as being generally supportive of Hart. Naturally just as Rice's "Monkey Business" revelations that were supposed to be helping Hart hurt him, this *Newsweek* article could also neatly be pointed to by Fiedler and the *Herald* when the paper came under fire for doing a hatchet job on the candidate.

The *Newsweek* article set the tone for everything that followed, and just as *Newsweek* clearly crossed the line between journalism and advocacy in this instance, it again did so much later when it called the "October Surprise" theories a myth in bold letters on its cover.
UPDATE: Although the contents of *Washington Post*'s investigation of Hart has not been and may never be released, sources have reported that they deal with the Senator's alleged relationship with another woman during a period of separation from wife, Lee.

CHAPTER SIX: A KINDER, GENTLER ASSASSINATION

Editors note: The original *The Gary Hart Set-Up* did not explain the meaning of the term "kinder, gentler assassination," because Bush's promise to usher in a "kindler, gentler' nation was an oft-used term of the Bush campaign.

The media had frequently compared the Hart campaign with the campaign of John F. Kennedy with good reason. Hart had demonstrated during his Senate years and earlier as an antiwar activist and McGovern campaign manager in 1972, that he, like Kennedy, would be a strong opponent to the covert activities of American intelligence agencies and the frequently resulting foreign entanglements.

Hart also disclosed that he fully understood the dangers of the Cold War and would seek to end it and the suicidal nuclear arms race that was an apparent result. If both Hart and John F. Kennedy were the victims of such covert actions, then, although the means differed considerably, the end result was the same. A President and an almost President who threatened an out-of-control netherworld of spooks, plots, intrigues, paranoia and dirty tricks ranging from mind control experimentation to murder were eliminated, thus paving the way for the ascension of more workable (and possibly quite intimidated) chief executives. The "operation" conducted against Hart might have been termed a "kinder, gentler assassination."

The Kennedy brothers were Gary Hart's heroes, role models and, in a sense, political mentors. It was, therefore, to be expected that when President Kennedy was assassinated that the effect on Hart would be dramatic and long-lasting. In fact, the assassination and perhaps even some of the assassins who escaped justice may well have shaped Hart's political career more than any other single factor.

Hart never believed the Warren Commission's version of the events at Dealey Plaza and was, in fact, an activist in seeking to force the government to release key evidence it held.

Was the assassination of President Kennedy the result of a covert action on the part of the professional intelligence community, as former CIA contract agent Robert Morrow, former CIA executive Victor Marchetti, former New Orleans District Attorney, Jim Garrison, and others have alleged or implied? If so, the assassination presumably was undertaken because of President Kennedy's alienation of the professional intelligence community and their allies, in particular, Kennedy's desire to break the CIA into a "thousand pieces." Compared to the nearly unthinkable assassination of a sitting President, then the prospect of derailing the campaign of a Presidential contender certainly would not present any insurmountable problems or moral dilemmas.

The professional intelligence community was allegedly an apparently loose confederation variously referred to as "the secret team," "the shadow government," or other stealth-like nomenclature.

….Despite the fact that no one in the intelligence community has yet been successfully prosecuted to their involvement in the Kennedy assassination and the constant threat of exposure regardless of the level of cover-up would tend to lend credence to the belief that the intelligence community may not have regarded the assassination as an overwhelming success. In terms of the loss of good agents alone the assassination was probably a greater disaster of the Bay of Pigs. Lee Harvey Oswald, Jack Ruby, Guy Bannister, Clay Shaw, David Ferrie, Count DeMohrenschildt, Sam Giancana, Johnny Roselli and a long list of others all may have died as a result of either what they might have known about the assassination. (A total of 50 individuals whose often mysterious deaths might be attributable to what they knew about the assassination were then listed. Some of the most notable of the 50 are:)

Lee Harvey Oswald, the accused assassin, murdered by Jack Ruby and who may have survived a murder attempt at the theater set up by a CIA contact at the theater.

Jack Ruby, claimed he was injected with cancer…linked to organized crime, placed phone call to Jimmy Hoffa at the time of the assassination.

Officer J.D. Tippit, murdered just after the Kennedy assassination, knew Ruby.

David Ferrie, victim of strange brain hemorrhage, CIA contract employee, knew Ruby and Oswald, worked for mobster Carlos Marcello.

Count George DeMohrenschildt, received a gunshot wound on the day that the Senate Intelligence committee located him (ruled a suicide), knew both Jackie Kennedy and Oswald.

Robert Perrin, arsenic poisoning, husband of Ruby employee, Nancy Perrin Rich. Perrin testified that Ruby was involved in Cuban arms smuggling deals.

Clyde Johnson, beaten the day before he was supposed to testify in Garrison's trial and murdered in a shotgun attack not long afterwards. Johnson knew of personal relationships between Clay Shaw, Ruby, Oswald and Ferrie.

Aladio del Valle, Shot and skull split open with a machete (killed the same hour as David Ferrie's strange brain hemorrhage). Valle was an anti-Castro exile whom Garrison was looking for as witness.

Bill Hunter, newspaper reporter who had been in Ruby's apartment on the night Ruby shot Oswald, shot to death in the Long Beach police station.

Jim Koethe, had been with Ruby the same night Ruby shot Oswald, killed by a karate chop to the neck when coming out of the shower.

Thomas Hank Killam, was the husband of Wanda Joyce Killam, knew and worked for Ruby, may have known Oswald. Killam told his brother, "I am a dead man, but I am running as far as I am going to run."

Dorothy Killgallen, was the columnist who attended the Ruby trial and died under mysterious circumstances the night before she planned to expose information that would break the assassination mystery "wide open."

Betty (Nancy Jane Mooney) McDonald, was found hung in her jail cell. Betty was at a party with the Oswalds and DeMohrenschildts, worked for Ruby, gave testimony that resulted in the release of Darrell Garner, who was accused of shooting Warren Reynolds. Reynolds had witnessed the Tippit shooting, following the killer for a block and swore it was not Oswald.

Marilyn April Walle, was shot to death. She also worked for Ruby and was planning on writing a book about the assassination.

Harold Russell, another witness to the escape of Tippit's killer, went "berserk" at a party saying he was going to be killed. Police were called to calm him. He was hit by a cop and died in January of 1967.

Richard Carr, stated that he had seen a heavy set man in a tan sportscoat and horn-rimmed glasses on the sixth floor of the depository just after the assassination saw two men run from behind the building, get into a Rambler and go north on Houston Street, and then saw the man in the sportscoat running away. He claimed to have been told by the FBI to keep his mouth shut and was harassed by the Dallas Police. He also received threatening calls, found a bomb in his car, testified at the Garrison trials in New Orleans. Carr died of a stab wound in Atlanta but managed to shoot and kill one of his Atlanta attackers.

Rose Cherrami, was one of Ruby's employees who had prior knowledge of the assassination, which she reported to the authorities after being thrown out of a moving car. She was finally killed by a hit and run driver in 1965.

Gary Underhill, was an ex-CIA agent and writer who fled Washington after telling friends that the CIA was involved in the assassination, was shot in what was described as execution style inexplicably ruled a suicide.

…Another set of similarities between the Kennedy assassination and the Hart affair are the obstacles confronting investigators of both events. These include both the secrecy that shrouds the truth as well as the drumbeat of establishment media (not all of whom could be accurately termed "propaganda assets,") which attacks the speculations and theories of investigators for not knowing what they are not allowed to know.

The trials and tribulations of the Garrison investigation into the Kennedy assassination have been replayed both literally and figuratively by Oliver Stone's movie *JFK*. Garrison found governmental interference, withholding of evidence and withholding of witnesses at every turn. An apparent spook offered Garrison a federal judgeship to drop the investigation. Because he would not play ball NBC attacked Garrison in a "white paper" documentary. The rest of the media followed suit and the government brought charges against Garrison for which he was eventually acquitted. Unfortunately the charges created disruption and bad publicity that caused Garrison to lose his bid for reelection as New Orleans District Attorney.

Stone faced similar media disparagement with *JFK*. *Newsweek* announced on its front cover that "JFK cannot be trusted." Former President (as well as former Warren Commission member) Gerald Ford attacked Stone in *New York Times*, as did nearly all of the media in unison.

The most vicious attack, however, came from conservative columnist and member of the *Washington Post* writers group, George Will. Will referred to the movie as a diatribe, a travesty and contemptible, calling Stone a man of "scant intelligence: and "arrested development" and even wondering aloud if it was ignorance or venality that caused Kevin Costner to play a part in the production.

…Fortunately, however, a few columnists and journalists have called for a fairer means of evaluating Stone's movie and charges. Alan Dershowitz, of United Features Syndicate, for example, states that if one is to condemn Stone's version of history in *JFK*, it would be intellectually dishonest not to condemn at the same time the massive suppression of evidence in the case and the tainted results of the Warren Commission.

In the case of the Kennedy assassination the missing or suppressed evidence includes CIA, FBI and other intelligence files on Oswals, bullet fragments from the "magic bullet," notes written by Oswald to the FBI, President Kennedy's brain, a film that may have been taken at the autopsy, the report of the Congressional committee investigating the assassination, etc.

In the case of the Hart affair, it is the identity of the informant to the *Miami Herald*, the identity of the

Washington Post's private investigator (and his report), the identity of the woman identified in the investigator's report, the fact that Rice herself will not talk with investigators and finally the contents of the government's files on Hart, Rice and Armandt.

UPDATE: Just as the Atwater deathbed confession proved to me and many others that the Hart affair was a set-up, the deathbed confession of E. Howard Hunt, proved that the Kennedy assassination was also the result of a conspiracy. Interestingly, the mainstream press has by and large ignored the explosive Hunt revelations.

The April 5, 2007 issue of *Rolling Stone* carried the deathbed confession of E. Howard Hunt, most notable as the Nixon White House conduit to the Watergate burglars entitled "The Last Confession of Howard Hunt." Hunt was also an admitted CIA operative connected with the events at the Bay of Pigs and with the anti-Castro Cuban underground.

The confession was taken by Hunt's son, Saint John Hunt over the course of several meeting. According to Hunt's confession LBJ himself gave the orders to a CIA hit team. LBJ used the Warren Commission in a mostly successful cover-up effort.

Involved with the hit team and/or cover-up, were Cord Meyer, CIA agent and husband of Mary Meyer with whom JFK may have been having an affair. Interestingly, Meyer was the primary force behind "Operation Mockingbird," which specialized in disinformation and which would have been very useful in any cover up attempts.

82

Also involved were Bay of Pigs veterans, some of whom were also connected with mob figures Sam Giancana and Santos Trifficante, David Atlee Phillips, William Harvey, Antonio Veciana, Frank Sturgis, David Morales and French Connection figure Lucien Sarti. Hunt revealed that Sarti was the second shooter on the Grassy Knoll. Sturgis and Hunt himself were identified by JFK conspiracy authors as two of the three "tramps" arrested at Dealey Plaza. The Hunt revelations made no mention of the possible roles of George H. W. Bush and Richard despite the fact that many conspiracy theories view their roles as pivotal.

It is certainly possible that while Hunt would be aware of the operations and personnel involved directly in the hit team, of which he had a part, and the roles of others which he could deduce, he might not have been privy to all of the players. After all, need to know is always the best way to conduct covert ops. It seems most likely that Hunt learning that LBJ had ordered the hit was a security slip-up.

CHAPTER SEVEN: MORE KENNEDY PARALLELS

...Although Hart was the manager of the disastrous McGovern campaign of 1972, the connection with the Kennedy assassination entangled him early in his independent political life. Hart may have alienated the still in power Kennedy assassins as early as 1974, when Nixon Attorney General John Mitchell ordered the Justice Department to block ballistics evidence from the Kennedy assassination on "national security" grounds. This evidence was the FBI's secret spectrographic analysis of the bullet and bullet fragments recovered...

Amazingly, the report disappeared from the National Archives. Harold Weisberg, an assassination investigator, sued for the report, which was partly responsible for a crucial amendment to the Freedom of Information Act in 1974, sponsored by none other than Senator Gary Hart.

Senator Ted Kennedy, during a Senate floor debate, asked Hart, "as I understand it the impact and effect of your amendment would be to override (the decision to deny access to the FBI study). Is that correct?"

Hart answered, "the Senator from Massachusetts is correct."

Kennedy replied, "then I support it." Clearly the prospect of a Hart presidency must have been unnerving to the Secret Team.

Hart may have been the victim of a CIA-sponsored assassination attempt as early as 1983. Hart had already made a name for himself by leading the opposition to the MX missile, as a member of the Church and Intelligence Committees, publicly doubting the Warren Commission and now poised not only to run for President but to lead the opposition to the Reagan Administration involvement in Central America.

On September 4, 1983, Hart and Senator William Cohen of Maine left Washington on an Air Force C-140 on a fact finding trip to Central America. Their initial destination was Managua, Nicaragua. About an hour out of Managua the pilot was advised that the airport had been attacked and the plane was re-routed to Honduras where it landed. The attackers flew a Cessna with 500 pound bombs under each wing and was flown by two Contra airmen. Among the areas most heavily damaged by the bombs was the VIP lounge where Cohen and Hart had scheduled a news conference. Cohen estimated that if he and Hart had been in the lounge before the scheduled press conference, they might have been killed. Air attacks against the Managua airport were hardly commonplace. The *New York Times* called the attack the first since 1979. Contra commander Eden Pastora, a.k.a. "Commander Zero" and his Contras took credit for the attack.

The pilot and co-pilot, both killed in the attack, left behind papers that left little doubt of the CIA sponsorship of their mission, but when Hart confronted the CIA station chief, he suggested the raid was initiated by Pastora.

Later, the CIA may have sponsored the infamous unsuccessful La Penca assassination attempt of Pastora that opened a can of worms for the agency, including allegations of CIA-sponsored cocaine smuggling activities in the United States.

The next day the Senators were in a helicopter in El Salvador when a hydraulic line suddenly began to rapidly lose pressure and the copter nearly crashed. When Hart returned to Washington, CIA Director William Casey invited Hart to his office to tell him that no one was really trying to kill him.

A second theory is that the near miss in Managua was intentional and intended to be a warning to Hart. In any event, because it was the Nicaraguans carrying out an attack in Nicaragua, the CIA had nothing to lose if Hart became "collateral damage." Plausible deniability is certainly high in such an operation, but whether the timing of the attack was coincidental or no Commander Zero is not saying. Pastora and the CIA later had a falling out due to his hesitance to become part of a unified Contra command and a bombing attempt was made on his life during a news conference, which is also widely assumed to have been orchestrated by the CIA.

Hart, however, may not have been completely satisfied with Casey's assurances that no one was trying to kill him. In his letter to us Hart stated that "The trip that Senator Cohen and I made to Central America in 1983 has been essentially accurately reported – but curiously underplayed – in the press."

By this does Hart mean to say that two very suspicious close calls (which were never really investigated) of a Senator, who was a known opponent of CIA involvement in Central America as well as vocal critic of the CIA itself who had just started to have Presidential aspirations, should have been considered more newsworthy? Did Hart suspect media ignorance or complicity? And why only now does he apparently feel either safe enough or reflective enough to comment publicly?

…. Another interesting parallel between the Hart affair and the Kennedy assassination has to do with the possible presence of a "second Donna Rice," as much as many Kennedy assassination theories revolve around a "second Oswald." The *Herald* account made mention of videotape that CBS aired, supposedly shot by tourists, which purported to show Hart on board the Monkey Business with an unidentified blonde woman who was not Donna Rice. That same videotape shows the same woman "strutting in bikini before a crowd of wolf whistlers during a hot bod contest at a south Florida bar." It appears that in the mad dash to add a dose of not too subtle sex to the Hart scandal, someone may have overdone it.

Since by all accounts the only passengers on the Monkey Business were Rice, Armandt, Broadhurst and Hart, why was a brand new blonde suddenly present? And why did tourists have, on the same videotape, that same young woman parading in a bar in a bikini? What are the odds that tourists would not only see the same young woman twice, but have camera ready on both occasions?

And if she was not Rice, could the "Hart" on the boat been a Hart lookalike? Why couldn't this woman be identified, despite the fact that she had performed in a bar and must have identified herself to someone in order to compete in a contest? Again the *Herald* and every other media outlet in the nation displayed an amazing lack of curiosity.

We wrote to CBS news hoping to obtain a copy of the video, which, of course, we offered to pay for. To date we have received no response, not even a rejection of our offer.

CHAPTER EIGHT: JUST SAY NO

According to James Hougan's *Spooks*, when Thai born CIA contract agent Puttaporn Khramkhruan was arrested in Chicago with 59 pounds of nearly pure opium, he was supposedly in the agency's employ as a "narcotics intelligence agent." Reasonable individuals might have expected the agency to feel betrayed that one of its own, employed for the use of spying on the drug trade of what is known as the Golden Triangle, was now caught with an enormous amount of street drugs with a value in the tens of millions and would no doubt want such an individual given the maximum sentence under the law.

Instead the CIA prevailed upon the Justice Department to drop the prosecution citing security reasons. It seems unlikely that this Thai contract agent could have known secrets so detrimental to the security of the nation that the government would be willing to overlook the matter of nearly 60 pounds of hard narcotics, yet this is not the only instance of mysterious duplicity on the part of the CIA when it came to drug smuggling into the United States. As noted earlier, just prior to his assassination Kennedy had called the CIA on the carpet concerning drug smuggling from the Golden Triangle.

The Christic Institute, an interfaith center for law and policy that performs legal investigations in the areas of social justice and human rights, has alleged that the covert Special Operations Group of the CIA located in Laos during the Vietnam war received kickbacks from narco-warlord Vang Pao, in addition to the agency's well documented connections with opium trafficking such as was depicted in the book and movie *Air America.*

…During the 1950s the CIA joined forces with the Corsican mob and other gangsters to break the Communist domination of unions in Marseilles, France, locale of the heroin processing labs, which would become the world-famous French connection. This was first speculated upon by Peter Scott, in his book *Cocaine Politics.* But his speculation was overshadowed when the highest ranking CIA official to ever go public, Victor Marchetti, in a recent interview confirmed that the overriding purpose behind the CIA alliance with the Corsican mob was to bring heroin into the US.

At the same time defeated Chinese nationalists, forced out of mainland China, were set up ostensibly for purposes of guerilla warfare against the communists in northern Burma. Unfortunately, as a military presence the nationalists were a joke, perhaps due to the fact that most of their efforts were directed at planting opium poppies and turning northern Burma into one of the most productive heroin producers in the world. It is arguable that without CIA transport of drugs out of remote northern Burma locations a market for the Burmese heroin could ever have developed.

According to Joseph Smith's *Portrait of a Cold Warrior,* Chinese nationalist General Li Mi commanded 1200 troops who escaped to Burma from Yunan province in the last days before the communist takeover.

Considering the millions in the communist Chinese army it becomes hard to imagine that the CIA would ever have a considered a force of just over 1000 anything more than a minimal potential nuisance for the communists.

The nationalist force quickly linked up with a Thai general named Pao who worked closely with a CIA cover corporation called SEA Supply Company. Pao also had extensive opium fields in northeastern Burma and a mutually beneficial relationship blossomed which allowed the Chinese to participate in the opium trade until 1961 when they were driven out of Burma.

From there the Chinese nationalists moved on to other parts of what would become the world's largest opium producing region during the Vietnam war, the Golden Triangle. The triangle consisted of eastern Burman northern Thailand and northern Laos. General Tuan Shi-wen, commander of the nationalist Chinese fifth army in northern Thailand quite candidly told the *Weekend Telegraph* of London, "We have to continue to fight the evil of communism, and to fight you must have an army, and an army must have guns, and to buy guns you must have money. In these mountains the only money is opium." CIA officer Des Fitzgerald considered the "operation" a high priority, and relations between the US and Burma were badly damaged as a result.

The CIA may also have assisted efforts by the anti-Soviet resistance in Afghanistan to use opium profits to fund their war. The opium was reportedly processed into heroin in Pakistan and, while it maintained a massive presence in

Pakistan, the DEA was prevented from moving or seeking to have the Pakistani government act against drug traffickers for "political reasons." During the decade of the 1980s it was estimated that nearly 75% of the world's heroin supply originated in Pakistan. Wisconsin professor Albert McCoy described how the CIA aided in drug money laundering through the Pakistani owned Bank of Commerce and Credit International (BCCI) and suggested that the BCCI was just one of a number of banks to whom the CIA and its partners in drug trafficking were able to turn to.

Among the CIA scandals brought out in the Senate and House hearings was the fact that the CIA had infiltrated a number of agents into the Bureau of Narcotics and Dangerous Drugs, the predecessor of the DEA, under the cover of an operation named "Project Merrimac." The CIA used the pretense of "monitoring any illegal activities of other BNDD employees." The scandal was supposed to be that the CIA was taking on responsibilities that more rightly belonged to the internal affairs section of the BNDD or were more properly (not to mention legally) the venue of the FBI in the event that the BNDD was considered corrupt beyond redemption.

No doubt some members of both agencies believed the CIA's pretense, but given the level of potential drug smuggling links that have been tied to the agency the infiltration could easily (and much more logically) be cast in a much more ominous light.

It could now become much easier for the agency to cover its own tracks, to head off embarrassing investigations before they started and to throw ongoing investigations off track with a combination of various sabotage, psychological warfare and disinformation techniques. It would also be helpful for smugglers working for or with the agency to know the identity of undercover BNDD operatives, knowledge that might well have led to the deaths of some informers.

Furthermore, the true nature of the conflict between the BNDD and the CIA became quite apparent in Laos in 1971. At the time Laos was one of the few nations in the world with no law against opium and opium trafficking. Perhaps the highest Laotian officials were involved in one way or another with the traffic, and CIA sponsored Meo tribesmen, who in their spare time harassed the Ho Chi Minh Trail, made their living growing opium. All of this had been a fairly comfortable arrangement until Laotian heroin began making its way to American GIs fighting in Vietnam. When that began to be widely reported the BNDD felt it had no choice but to attempt to stop the tide of heroin at its source in Laos.

The State Department and the CIA, however, were able to prevent the BNDD from even opening an office in Laos for months until the intervention of then-President Nixon and the first "war on drugs" forced a change. At that point the agency suggested to the Laotians that it would be to all of their benefits to appear to begin to appear to be cooperating in the drug war. The Laotian government responded with an anti-drug crusade aimed, mostly if not exclusively, at harassing addicts, since any major offensive whose goal it was to put an actual end to drug production and trafficking would obviously target the Laotian government itself.

Thus, a cynical Laotian "war on drugs" was born, effectively doubling the misery of the individual addicts but allowing the flow of narcotics to continue unimpeded while placating the political concerns of Washington. With some modifications this remains the model for drug fighting to date.

It is further noted that, just as Colombian cocaine began to replace heroin as the drug of choice on the streets, the CIA would again find itself involved in a clandestine war effort convenient for the transshipment of drugs into the country. The clandestine machinery that transported weapons to the anti-Communist tribesmen of Indochina, as well as the Contras of Central America could also provide an excellent cover for the lucrative narcotics trade. This drug trade could be taken advantage of by both greedy agents and/or an agency eager to secure sources of funding that were both untraceable and untouchable. It then becomes clear the agency would feel threatened not only by opposition to its trade by those in the know but by opposition to the intervention that made the trade itself possible as well.

Kennedy appeared to have been in the process of becoming an opponent to the…CIA's role in Indochina. Hart was also an outspoken adversary of the nation's and the agency's roles in Nicaragua.

CHAPTER NINE: THE BOULDER-MIAMI CONNECTION

A number of things culminated in late 1991, the last of which was the nationwide release of Oliver Stone's film *JFK* on December 20, 1991.

…Even before *JFK*'s release, we had made the decision to go ahead with a very general article about the Hart set-up, largely out of concerns for our safety. The "suicide" of investigative reporter Danny Casolaro in West Virginia had made us aware that the government apparently had decided that hostile investigative reporters were legitimate targets. Casolaro had been investigating the INSLAW case, in which it was alleged that the Justice Department stole software useful in monitoring "dissidents."

It was also rumored that Casolaro was working on the "October Surprise" allegations, in which the Reagan campaign was accused of negotiating with the Iranian government to have the American hostages held until Reagan was inaugurated in order to sabotage the Carter campaign. Whatever the case, Casolaro was well aware that he was in significant danger and told his family not to believe any "accident" that might occur.

Casolaro had been scheduled to meet with an extremely sensitive source in a hotel room in West Virginia. Instead Casolaro was found dead of what was officially ruled suicide in that hotel room. Suspicious circumstances included the fact that Casolaro was said to have sliced his wrists down to the tendons. Suicides who slice their wrist usually show hesitation marks and usually slice just deeply enough for bleeding to commence. They usually do not wish to inflict more pain than is necessary and slicing down to the tendons was likely extremely painful. Also suspicious was the fact that the police disposed of the body before the family could be notified.

Casolaro was certainly not the first investigative reporter to die in the line of duty, and certainly will not be the last. …We felt that we had enough information to make any reasonable person conclude that, given the body of evidence (or lack thereof), there was reason to suspect that there was more to the Hart-Rice affair than met the eye. We had already obtained letters from Ben Bradlee at the *Washington Post* and Tom Fiedler at the *Miami Herald*, (please see appendicies) but we did not want to go around asking the wrong people questions before having some kind of "insurance." We felt the best insurance would be a general article which asked enough questions to arouse the public's curiosity, but which used no facts that could not be verified and cross referenced from a number of sources.

We decided to do a good deal of tiptoeing around speculation as to what might really have happened and in naming specific names, especially due to Armandt's lawsuit against the authors of *Blue Thunder*. Aside from attacking the discrepancies that seemed to exist in the "official story," the article centered primarily on the roles of the mass media and the question of whether or not they might have been witting or unwitting propaganda assets.

The article was copyrighted with an original sent back to the authors as well as a copy to *Playboy* magazine as it was felt that 1) the article's appearance in *Playboy* would garner the most attention for us, 2) *Playboy* did not appear to be a propaganda asset and therefore we thought could be counted upon to give the article fair treatment and 3) *Playboy* paid better than anyone else.

We were, therefore, very surprised to receive a response from *Playboy* Senior Editor Peter Moore stating that *Playboy* had been engaged in writing just such an article since the summer and that a pair of its writers were completing the research "as we speak." (We later spoke to Moore and he told us that the article had been 'put on hold' until at least the August issue.) The letter went on to say that the magazine was returning the article "unread" but that we might be able to get a consultancy on the *Playboy* article by calling Sally Denton, one of the *Playboy* article's authors.

We received the *Playboy* response on a Friday afternoon. Our first assumption was that *Playboy* was lying, that they had read the article and just planned to steal it, offering us a pittance for our efforts. On Monday, however, Blake called Denton in New Mexico. The conversation was very interesting, both to us and what we would now refer to as "the other team." Denton said that she was the author of *The Bluegrass Conspiracy* and that the *Playboy* team had a source, who was described as someone in federal law enforcement who claimed to be "the guy who did the job (on Hart)." Properly impressed, we were nonetheless confused about the "other team" not seeming to know some of the basic facts, including the Armandt lawsuit.

97

Later in analyzing what we learned from the call to Denton, we wondered if our policy of not referring to anonymous sources for any information whatsoever would handicap us in competing with the "other team." We made this policy in response to the accusations made against Bob Woodward and the doubt surrounding his "Deep Throat" source, as well as the fact that the *Herald* tip regarding the Hart affair had come from an "anonymous source" whose identity the *Herald* still refuses to disclose. It was our feeling that we could not credibly criticize the *Herald*'s actions if we also relied on just such an unfair and less than credible information source.

We were reassured, however, that the *Playboy* team was for real and that, in fact, the magazine may have acted amazingly ethically given the circumstances. Denton said that she would pass on our phone number to the senior editor at *Playboy* and see if we might be able to come to some sort of cooperative arrangement rather than have two teams engaging in a race over one blockbuster story. Denton told us that her team was looking at a June publication date. We worried that this might be an attempt to get us relaxed into thinking we had a big lead on the "other team."

We were very relieved, however, to discover that other investigative reporters were working on the story, and we no longer felt that we were the enormous targets we had once perceived ourselves to be. We were disturbed, however, by a speculated possibility that the "other team's" source may be feeding them some disinformation, as some of the overall theories they now were entertaining seemed somewhat at odds with the facts we had so far discovered.

Later we received a call from Ken Cummins, who identified himself as Denton's partner on the article....Blake...was very uncomfortable with the call. Cummins stated that the *Playboy* team had conducted some but not all of the interviews necessary and that they would need to go to England for another interview. He stated that a byline for us was not possible but offered to pay $300 just to read our article. Later we...felt it would be fine for them to send $300 to read the article and called Cummins to say that was agreeable. Cummins stated that he would be mailing the $300 that day. The promised $300 never arrived.

Getting nowhere with *Playboy* we decided to go ahead and see if we could get the article published locally in the Denver area. A friend suggested trying *Westword,* a free weekly newspaper that bills itself as an "Arts and Entertainment Weekly."

The paper had once gone out on a limb to report a suspected affair between Colorado Governor Roy Romer and his female chief of staff. The paper was widely assailed for that, as well as a subsequent article exposing that the late University of Colorado quarterback, Sal Aunese, was also the father of coach Bill McCartney's unmarried daughter's child. Again the paperwas roundly booed by the local media. It seemed logical, therefore, to approach *Westword* with the Hart article.

What we did not expect, however, was the editor's expressed aversion for "conspiracy theories," and an apparent personal animosity towards Hart. *Westword* Editor Patricia Calhoun wrote us that she knew Gary Hart had tried to pick up *Westword*'s national advertising representative in New York and stated that she had the note to prove it. We felt that Calhoun had missed the point – we were not asserting that Hart was a saint – but in any event, we requested a copy of the note…Calhoun responded that the woman who had it had no interest in making the note public or she would have done so long ago.

…Undaunted, we next submitted the article to *Denver Magazine*. Editor Nancy Clark was extremely excited about the article. Clark said that she planned to use the article in the March issue…it seemed as though the article would (finally) be seeing print.

Ironically, however, just days before the March issue would have gone to press, Mrs. Clark called to let us know that after 22 years *Denver Magazine* had suddenly gone out of business. There would be no March issue. Clark told Blake that she was unaware of any financial problems at the magazine and, in fact, felt that it had been doing better than ever.

…Another newspaper that we attempted to interest in the story was the *Boulder Daily Camera*. We speculated that the other Denver area dailies, the *Rocky Mountain News* and the *Denver Post* were too connected to either the *Herald* (in the case of the *Rocky Mountain News*) or the

Washington Post (in the case of the *Denver Post*) and that the *Camera* might be more inclined to give it a fair hearing. We were again surprised when the editor of the *Camera* informed us that he felt the story was not new and that the same story had been carried earlier. Having thoroughly researched the story, we were sure that this was not the case, but we did not give it much thought and went back to work on the book.

Later we contacted the *Colorado Daily,* the University of Colorado's student newspaper, attempting to interest them in a short article concerning the issues raised in the book. Once again we were met at first with enthusiasm. We were referred to reporter Chris Wolf, who was at first quite interested in pursuing the story but then inexplicably began backing away. Fortunately, however, we were not only able to salvage some information from Mr. Wolf, which helped to explain his (and probably other's) hesitancy to look seriously into the issue, but which also opened an entirely new window on the secret history of America.

On the day that Wolf informed us that he probably did not want to use the article or one done by himself on the same subject, Wolf mentioned that he knew something about what the *Camera* may have turned down the article. Additionally, he told us he knew of a former *Camera* publisher who had moved to Miami to a take a job at the *Herald,* where she died shortly thereafter. Some had speculated that she died "under mysterious circumstances" possibly because of what she knew about the Hart affair. He gave Blake the name and phone number of a doctor of internal medicine named Robert McFarland who, he was told, had a great deal of information on the subject.

Blake called McFarland and was amazed at not only what McFarland knew, but just how willing he seemed to be to talk and the remarkable accuracy of his recollections when the verifiable facts were checked. McFarland began by stating that the former *Camera* employee sent to Miami was Janet Chusmire (possibly spelled Chusmir), then publisher of the *Camera*. She had died later that same year of an "intercerebral hemorrhage," which McFarland did not think was a result of the Hart affair. At the *Herald* Chusmire became the editor. She also had taken one of her reporters, Martin Connelly, with her. Connelly is currently in Kansas City, having left the *Herald* shortly after Chusmire's death.

On some issues we clearly doubted the accuracy of McFarland's theories. For example, he speculated that Hart had allowed himself to be caught with Donna Rice to avoid being caught with laundered money from BCCI. We doubted this was the case. However, a former aide to Hart had stated that the campaign was totally dependent on loans from First American Bank, a bank later connected to BCCI for a period of more than a year.

Also interesting was McFarland's theory as to why Chusmire had been promoted to the Miami newspaper in the first place. McFarland was the former director of the Boulder Methadone clinic and as a result became somewhat of a local expert on heroin addicts and heroin trafficking. In 1984 a local addict turned in a heroin laboratory located in nearby Longmont to the local sheriff's department and district attorney's office.

What made the laboratory unique was that until that time heroin had usually been processed in foreign locales, especially Marseilles, France – the location of the French connection and the fact that it was located in the facility of a military contractor with top secret clearance.

The addict had been a long time friend of the man responsible for the lab. The addict felt that the head of the lab was a long-time CIA operative. When Boulder County authorities appeared to be dragging their feet on investigating the lab, the addict took the story to the *Camera*, which, in a pattern that seemed very familiar to us, was at first enthused and then suddenly did an about face and seemed to do everything possible to squelch the story. The *Colorado Daily* also backed off the story when McFarland and the addict approached them.

McFarland believed that Chusmire was promoted to the *Herald* as a reward for sitting on the heroin lab story. The *Herald* had already established a track record of cooperating with the CIA when it sat on the story of Cuban exile bases before it was scooped by other newspapers. Additionally, Joe Calhoun, an investigative reporter who was covering the trial of former Panamanian strongman, Manuel Noreiga, reported that the *Herald* was spiking articles about the trial that might have proved embarrassing to the government.

Then Congressman Tim Wirth paid attention to the allegations, however. On September 8, 1984, Wirth publicly called for a Congressional investigation into the role that the DEA had played in the heroin lab affair.

103

Wirth noted that the addict, Paul McGuirk, informed the DEA as early as 1981 of the lab's existence.

No arrest was made in the case until a janitor inadvertently discovered the lab in 1984, and the head of the lab, Sandy Jones, was arrested in July of that year…Not surprisingly no Congressional hearing was ever conducted…and Wirth went on to become a US Senator in 1986.

In fact, only one formal Congressional investigation into the connection between US intelligence agencies and narcotics trafficking has ever occurred. Those were the hearings chaired by Senator John Kerry of Massachusetts, chairman of the Subcommittee on Terrorism, Narcotics and International Operations, in December of 1988. The hearings were extremely poorly covered by the mass media and the committee's recommendations were, for the most part, ignored. The hearings were allowed to occur because of the peripheral relationship of the Contra-cocaine connection to the more widely heralded Iran-Contra scandal.

To many…the most widely held impression of the Iran-Contra scandal was the flamboyant testimony of Lt. Colonel Oliver North, a figure many regarded as a hero…the media did not discourage this perception. How many would still regard North as a hero had the contents of North's journal, reprinted in the Kerry Subcommittee report, been made more public?

The following are excerpts of North's journal, from page 151 of the report:

"June 26, 1984 – Call from Owen-John Hull protection. John has a private army of 75-100 Cubans involved in drugs—up to 100 more Cubans expected."

July 20, 1984 – Call from Claridge: Alfredo Cesar re drugs—Borge-Owen leave Hull alone."

August 9, 1985 – (following a meeting with Robert Owen) DC-6 which is being used for runs out of New Orleans is probably being used for drug runs into the US.

Despite Fawn Hall's testimony that she spent a considerable amount of time shredding documents in North's office, clearly all of the potentially incriminating material was not destroyed. If North felt these entries were innocuous, one wonders what was shredded that would have been more incriminating than this. Curiously, North was never indicted with what would certainly have been the most serious charge related to Iran-Contra, aiding and abetting narcotics trafficking into the US.

…Unfortunately, despite the fact that the Subcommittee conducted 14 days of testimony that touched on a government scandal that dwarfed Watergate, nine executive sessions were held, casting doubt on whether the Subcommittee could truly come clean with the American people on the level of government complicity in the narcotics trade.

Unsurprisingly, other government agencies were less than completely cooperative with the Subcommittee. Appendix B of the Kerry report is entitled "Allegations of Interference with the Committee Investigation," and states that "...the Subcommittee received sworn testimony from an assistant US attorney that officials in the Justice Department sought to undermine the attempts by Senator Kerry to have hearings on the allegations."

McFarland alleges that Kerry "backed off" when the going got rough, and the watered down conclusions of the Subcommittee seem to bear him out.

For example, on page 36 the report states that the Contra drug links included:

> "Involvement in narcotics trafficking by individuals associated with the Contra movement."
> "Participation of narcotics traffickers in Contra supply operations through business relationships with Contra organizations."
> "Provision of assistance to the Contras by narcotics..."
> "Payments to drug traffickers by the US State Department of funds authorized by the Congress."

The conclusions of the Subcommittee downplay these findings and state only that "there are serious questions as to whether or not US officials involved in Central America failed to address the drug issue for fear of jeopardizing the war effort against Nicaragua."

...Later when John Hull, who was widely acknowledged to be a CIA agent in Costa Rica and an important player in Kerry's investigation, became the focus for an FBI investigation into cocaine trafficking through Central America, US officials in Costa Rica were quick to jump to Hull's defense. In what is perhaps the best example of an official governmental explanation for the protection of certain narcotics operations, a US embassy security officer told one of the FBI agents that Hull was an employee of a government agency with "different operational requirements." Those requirements were, of course, the maintenance of an extensive narcotics operation on a worldwide basis.

McFarland also talked about the alleged connections between George Bush, Neil Bush and convicted drug smuggler Marcello Cabus, Jr., that were contained in an article by Bryan Abas in the July 13, 1988 issue of *Westword*. Abas has since left *Westword* and McFarland noted that *Westword* had taken a great deal of heat for the article and was now backing off of anything resembling the allegations contained in the Abas article.

Perhaps the most interesting assertion that the article made was that a top federal law enforcement officer approached the chief federal prosecutor for Colorado, Robert Miller, with information that he had an informant who knew of the link between the Bushes and Cabus, but that the informant was understandably nervous. Miller listened politely and as the officer was leaving he noticed a note on Miller's desk signed by Neil Bush, reminding Miller of their dinner engagement that evening. Needless to say there is no evidence that the investigation was ever pursued and the informant wisely chose to quit talking.

…An even more unsettling conversation involved McFarland, McGuirk and Joe Kelso. Kelso, who claimed to be a CIA contract agent was also mentioned in Oliver North's journals and had been arrested for selling missiles to Iraq. McFarland…brought up the subject of the murder of Swedish Prime Minister Olaf Palme, wondering aloud if the still unsolved murder might have carried out by the agency. Indeed, that was the case, Kelso told him, adding that he had been in Amsterdam where the assassination was planned…

UPDATE: *San Jose Mercury News* reporter Gary Webb, who together with his main source, crack dealer "Freeway Ricky Ross" exposed the Contra-Cocaine connection allegedly committed suicide. Instead of receiving a well deserved Pulitzer Prize, Webb was found dead, having allegedly shot himself in the head, <u>twice</u>.
It almost seemed as though Webb's killers knowingly shot him in the head twice, knowing that the fix was in and his death would be declared a suicide even if he had had his hands tied behind his back. The purpose of that would serve as a message to other investigative reporters, we can kill you and get away with it.

CHAPTER TEN: A PRIMER FOR THE INTELLIGENCE OPERATIVE: HOW TO BUY, RIG AND SABOTAGE AN ELECTION OR CAMPAIGN

The democratic process is inherently vulnerable to manipulation by covert activity. In addition to the previously mentioned instances of covert CIA interference in the elections of France, Italy and Chile, the CIA has also interfered in the elections in the Philippines, Ecuador and Indonesia. And in what may well be an excellent example of a violation of its charter, the Puerto Rican independence movement has repeatedly charged the agency with intervention in Puerto Rican elections.

….In addition to simply providing campaign aid to the parties that the covert operators support, planting favorable or even "black propaganda" in local news outlets. Political campaigns and elections are extremely "soft" targets for almost any covert operation. Most successful campaigns have specialists in the areas of opposition research, intelligence, counter intelligence, political sabotage and counter sabotage.

…It is extremely easy to infiltrate an American… political campaign…The more successful a campaign has been in terms of inspiring the popular imagination the more obvious a target it becomes and the ease with which it can be infiltrated is increased.

One big reason is the presence and need to volunteers in a political campaign as well as the chaos in the campaign

109

office that this usually creates. If a large number of volunteers is coming into the office to do a few hours work on phone banks, mailing, posting and distributing campaign literature, it becomes a practical impossibility to do any sort of background investigation or check the identities and histories of the all the volunteers…

If a hostile political campaign can get an agent to pose as a volunteer the potential for damage…is enormous…The agent can, for instance, attempt to get close to the candidate for the purposes of creating a scandal…the agent can conduct ideological sabotage, attempting to get the candidate to endorse…unpopular positions designed to alienate voters…(or) conduct espionage activities, i.e., "digging up dirt" on the candidate or the campaign.

Another vulnerability with most campaign offices are the loose security precautions taken both with vital campaign documents (in Hart's case, copies of his stump speeches were found in the safe of drug smuggler Ben Kramer) and blank campaign stationary.

…These are only a few examples of the literally hundreds of possibilities for campaign sabotage and espionage that are present in any large campaign for national or significant state office. A target so "soft" and yet so potentially important would present tremendous temptations and opportunities for a sophisticated intelligence apparatus. It is a temptation that has not been resisted.

CHAPTER ELEVEN: THE 1992 CAMPAIGN

…The stronger political opposition was on the Democratic ticket, just as there had been in 1988. Former Arkansas Governor, Bill Clinton, quickly became the Democratic front runner…Early on in the campaign, rumors of womanizing on the part of the candidate began to circulate. This time the femme fatale was Gennifer Flowers, a part-time nightclub singer, with whom Clinton may have had a dalliance in the past. When Flowers would not tell her story to the mainstream media, the tabloids began making offers. Ultimately, Flowers was paid by the *Star* for her story…Amazingly the Flowers story blew over. Although the story had eventually made its way to the mainstream media and undercut some Clinton support…by and large the Clinton-Flowers affair was nothing like the Hart-Rice affair. The public had been primed for such a media display of the sordid details of a political candidates's sex life…and the womanizing accusations did not seem nearly as surprising or improper to the American people as they had five years earlier.

Another major difference between the Hart-Rice affair and the Clinton-Flowers affair was that Hillary Clinton, herself a lawyer and a formidable political adversary, immediately went on camera and "stood by her man," while claiming she was not doing so. On the other hand Lee Hart had mounted a much less vigorous defense of her husband to the point that rumors arose that she was leaving the Senator.

…Then there was allegations in the "alternative" press that Clinton had participated in a cover-up of the Contra cocaine connection at the Mena, Arkansas airport. Tabloid television programs such as "Now It Can Be Told," Geraldo Rivera's investigative news show, broadcast the allegations of Mena locals who asserted that the remote airfield was used not only to supply the Contras in Nicaragua with weapons, but that return flights were loaded with as much as 300 pounds of cocaine.

A courageous local group of Mena residents, known as the "Arkansas Committee," have held press conferences and issued press releases stating that the visitors to the airport included Oliver North and notorious cocaine smuggler Barry Seal. One CIA pilot, Richard Brenneke, claimed to have looked into boxes that he was carrying back to Mena and found what he believed to be cocaine. When he asked an official in Vice President Bush's office what was going on, was told to "mind his own business and just fly the plane."

Residents complained to reporters that they had been threatened and a state investigator may have been poisoned with "military grade biological warfare agents – Anthrax."

Investigators also approached Clinton's office with their allegations and claimed that they were ignored and in one case said that Clinton had offered $25,000 to investigate the Mena affair, an amount that the state investigator maintained was a mere fraction of what would be needed to launch such an investigation.

CHAPTER 12: A LINK TO THE ARONOW MURDER

"Don Aronow was a local celebrity in Miami. To fans of speedboat racing he was a living legend. His friends included kings (most notably King Hussein of Jordan) and (future) Presidents (most notably President Bush). Bush characterized himself as a close friend of Aronow's and owned an Aronow designed boat. To aid (in) the drug war Bush was instrumental in having the U.S. Customs order a number of Aronow's boats to use in drug interdiction.

It was also well known that drug smugglers were fans of the boats as well, often paying for them with suitcases full of cash. The fact that smugglers often used Aronow boats was well known to the DEA as well, and on February 3, 1987, just three months prior to withdrawal of Gary Hart from the Presidential campaign , full-time DEA surveillance was called off at Aronow's showroom and factory. Just a few hours later Don Aronow was murdered gangland style in the very same location.

People magazine, the Miami Herald and the controversial book *Blue Thunder* (which, as stated earlier, has been sued by Donna Rice's friend Lynn Armandt) all covered the investigation into Aronow's murder, certainly one of the most curious cases in recent memory.

To begin with, (following Aronow's murder) then Vice-President Bush began to immediately distance himself from the Aronow family, not attending the funeral of his 'close friend,' and refusing to acknowledge Aronow's widow in public. Aronow friends commented that the Vice President was "feeling guilty about something."

Next investigators tied Aronow to Meyer Lansky's nephew, Ben Kramer, and perhaps other smugglers, mobsters and money launderers. Witnesses appeared to be trying to throw police off the track and trusted friends of Aronow's widow seemed more interested in damage control than in finding out who murdered Aronow and why.

Perhaps more interesting, however, was the apparent connection between Aronow and Donnie Soffer, owner of Turnberry Isle Resort and the yacht "Monkey Business." Interesting also is the fact that Soffer was apparently the employer of both Lynn Armandt and Donna Rice, who Blue Thunder characterized as "party girls' hired to entertain and 'date' the rich clients of Turnberry. Another and perhaps even more significant connection, according to Blue Thunder, was the fact that Armandt's husband, alleged to be a drug dealer working with the same Ben Kramer, with whom Aronow had been partners, was also an apparent gangland style murder victim. Armandt's husband's car was found filled with machine gun holes and blood, although his body has never been recovered.

Blue Thunder theorized that Aronow had been killed because he was about to be subpoenaed by a grand jury and someone was worried that he might talk. The Blue Thunder authors apparently considered the Hart affair unrelated, but they quote a 'fed' as stating that the Hart affair was a set-up, organized by the mob.

With Aronow's connections it seems reasonable to conclude that one of the things he might have known about and therefore have been able to talk about was the Gary Hart set-up. It also seems strange that a 'fed' is accusing the mob of the set up, which brings to mind the various 'false sponsor' stratagems Kennedy assassination investigators have encountered.

Might the investigation into the Aronow murder bring the Gary Hart set-up to light? Those who are cynical may not be too surprised claim to have solved the case in a neat and tidy fashion. An inmate wanting release from prison recounted a tale allegedly told to him by another inmate, whom, he claimed , had Aronow killed at the behest of Colombian drug lords. The Colombian drug lords were angered at being stiffed on a cocaine deal by Aronow and Jeb Bush, another son of the President.

After dropping the Bush name from the charges, a grand jury issued an indictment for the other inmate who was already serving time for murder and a variety of other crimes. This appeared to be all too neat concluded Blue Thunder. Never mind that no eyewitness could identify the inmate as the killer and that he in no way resembled the composites of the witnesses. Never mind the inmate informer had nearly every other detail of the murder incorrect. Case closed.

UPDATES AND ADDITIONS

Blue Thunder also reported that Ben Kramer was also found in possession of a copy of Gary Hart's stump speech. Robert Young and Ben Kramer, both already doing life sentences, eventually pleaded "no contest" to the Aronow murder charges. Young was allowed to plead to second degree murder and thus avoided a possible death sentence.

In 2007 *Miami Beach 411.com* wrote a piece entitled *The Murder of Speedboat Builder Don Aranow*, which agreed with *Blue Thunder's* assessment. Matt Meltzer posed the question thusly, "Two guys who already were spending most if not all of their lives behind bars pleading to a crime nobody could solve? Seems a little too convenient." *Miami Beach 411* would add to the impressive list of Aronow contacts, to include Meyer Lansky himself, King Hussein of Jordan, Baby Doc Chevalier in Haiti, and former President Lyndon Johnson. The article referred to the Aronow murder as "the most sensational and drawn-out murder case in Miami history…"

After all, the article noted, Aronow, a millionaire at 28, "had gained worldwide fame" for developing the famous Cigarette boats that are "….still the generic name used for any, large high powered speed vessel," and was considered the "King of Thunderboat Row."

Both fortunately and unfortunately for Aronow "The combination of his location in the drug smuggling hub of North America that was Miami and his penchant for making the fastest, toughest boats in the world made him an obvious vendor for the nefarious characters who populated our region. His boats were the vessel of choice for dope smugglers bring product into South Florida, and Aronow was well aware of his reputation."

Aronow, "In order to make up for his contribution to the crime wave…built a series of boats for the Drug Enforcement Agency and Customs officials called Blue Thunder. These boats were faster and more powerful that the models being used by the drug runners and were applauded by the government as a valuable tool in the war on drugs. It was no coincidence that among the first riders in the Blue Thunder was then-Vice President Bush himself."

As what is known concerning the day of the Aronow murder, the article reports that "On the afternoon of February 3, 1987, Don Aronow as in his office on Thunderboat Row when a tall stranger walked in and identified himself as Jerry Jacoby. Jacoby claimed to work for a very rich man who wanted Aronow to build him a 60 foot boat…(memorably Jacoby stated that for his employer he would)…do anything for him….even kill for him."

When Aronow "prepared to leave the office, the tall stranger abruptly left." Arnow then "…drove his white Mercedes a few blocks to the offices of Apache Performance boats and his former protégé Robert Saccenti. After a brief social meeting Aronow drove out and was approached by a dark Lincoln Continental with tinted windows. The driver exchanged some words with Aronow and then shot him several times…"

Aronow was discovered by friend Bobby Moore shortly thereafter. Initial searches for Jacoby were unfruitful and other investigative avenues yielded little of value despite the fact that Aronow's widow, Lillian, offered a $100,000 reward for information leading to the arrest of his killers. *Miami Beach 411* went on to note that: "For years after the crime, the Miami-Dade homicide division kept all of its information top-secret.

As a result, the public and media developed a variety of theories as to why Aronow was killed...." ranging from jealous husbands or lovers to the mob to Aronow's cooperation with authorities, to a theory that authorities were using speedboat purchases to build a tax evasion case against drug smugglers. However, *Miami Beach 411* made no mention of Aronow's possible involvement in and/or knowledge of the Hart affair.

Ben Kramer, a convicted drug smuggler, nephew of Meyer Lansky and owner of a copy of the Hart stump speech, became a suspect because of his dealings with Aronow. According to *Miami Beach 411* "Kramer was a rival boat builder and racer who had purchased USA Racing Team from Aronow in 1984. In exchange for the company, Kramer gave Aronow land, assets, a helicopter and some cash. Cash that was, apparently under the table. When the company was sold, it was in the process of developing Blue Thunder for the federal government.

They, of course, believed USA Racing was still owned by Aronow. When the Feds found out he had sold the company to Kramer, they began to second guess their contractural arrangement with the company. Kramer, you see, was convicted in 1978 of smuggling large amounts of marijuana and distributing it throughout the United States. Not exactly the sort of guy Uncle Sam likes to do business with. At least not publicly."

Aronow hoped to save the contract with the government by purchasing the company back from Kramer, but, according apparently lost out on the deal, for, according to *Miami Beach 411*: "The generally-believed story among those on Thunderboat row is that Aronow returned the land, assets and helicopter, but kept the undocumented cash."

If true, this would give Kramer motive and "Miami-Dade investigators looked hard into Kramer, who again had been indicted on drug charges shortly after the Aronow killing, but could not make any leads stick. The case became a long drawn out whodunit."

Meanwhile in Oklahoma, an inmate arrested in a drug trafficking case, wanted for murder and attempted murder in Florida and labelled a "career criminal," by *Miami Beach 411* named Robert Young had allegedly told other inmates that he was the triggerman in the Aronow hit. Interestingly, when examining the background of Young, the name Jerry Jacoby, the name the mysterious stranger who appeared at the Aronow offices just prior to his assassination, appears.

"Among his other aforementioned contributions to society, Young had also once been convicted of smuggling drugs to Cuba. He was caught and thrown in prison, only to be released in 1984 in a bold political move by then

119

Presidential hopeful Jesse Jackson. Among those not freed: Young's partner in his ill-fated dope smuggling trip, Jerry Jacoby. It is not known whether this is the same man who walked into Aronow's office the day he was killed, but it has long been suspected that there were two shooters involved in the crime."

In their search for a co-conspirator, Miami authorities continued to focus on Kramer, a focus that had been frustrated until Kramer's former attorney, who had been convicted on and serving time for drug smuggling charges himself, Marvyn Kessler, informed investigators that in violation of his oath as an attorney he would "…testify that Kramer implicated himself in the 1987 Aronow shooting." In 1990 Young was charged with Aronow's murder although authorities refused to disclose whether or not they felt Young acted alone. At the time Young "…was already serving time for the "Dixie Mafia" murder and the Craig Marshall shooting…"

It wasn't until 1993 that Kramer was indicted "…who like Young, was serving a life sentence for his drug conviction. Because of his escape attempts (which once included a helicopter), however, he got to serve his time in Dade County Jail rather than the more pushily accommodated federal facility. His indictment was the most heavily guarded in the history of the Dade County Courthouse, inviting dogs, federal agents, aviation support and bomb searches."

Young was the first to fall when "In October 1995, ….Young finally pled 'no contest' to second degree murder, sparing him the possibility of a death sentence and, more importantly, keeping him from having to testify against Kramer....The deail also allowed the defendant to possibly be out of prison before he died..."

On the other hand prosecutors worried that the case against Kramer "...began to weaken. Marvyn Kessler's testimony...was ruled inadmissible as attorney-client privilege....(and) The rest of the case was based on testimony from inmates and phone conversations, not exactly an airtight conviction."

"Fortunately for prosecutors, the horrid conditions in Dade County Jail eventually forced Kramer's hand...the sub-freezing temperatures...the lack of bedding or even beds for that matter caused Ben Kramer eventually plead no contest to the same second degree murder charge that Young had pled to and, like Young was sentenced to 19 years. Kramer's attorney Jose Quinon stated that Kramer's plea was not an admission of guilt, although "for the Aronow family, it gave them some closure."

Was it just too neat that two inmates already doing life sentence confessed to a high profile gangland style murder that had evaded solution for years? Whether or not the Aronow murder was integral to or peripheral to the Hart affair, *Miami Beach 411* concludes by wondering "Will we ever know what really happened that February day in 1987? Thanks to a couple of No Contest pleas, probably not. But in a world populated by boat racers, drug dealers, mobsters and world leaders, anything is possible. And, more importantly, anything is possible to cover up.

APPENDICIES

LETTER TO THE *ATLANTIC*
LETTER TO *WESTWORD*

THE *METROPOLITAN ACCENT* ARTICLE
"WAS GARY HART SET UP?"

LETTERS FROM:

GARY HART,

BEN BRADLEE OF THE *WASHINGTON POST*

PLAYBOY MAGAZINE

TOM FIEDLER OF THE *MIAMI HERALD*

SUBSEQUENT *METROPOLITAN ACCENT* ARTICLES

"SPIES ON THE COLORADO FRONT RANGE"

"BLOOD MOON RISING: GLOBAL SATANISM COMES TO TOWN"

LETTER TO THE ATLANTIC

VINDICATION!! GARY HART WAS SET UP AND WE KNEW THAT WAS THE CASE BY 1992

In 1992, as a freelance Colorado based investigative reporter, I co-authored a book entitled *The Gary Hart Set-up*. The book has been out of print for years although I am seriously thinking of reissuing it given the new evidence. In fact what we had in 1992 was a huge amount of circumstantial evidence, but no deathbed confession. Among the circumstantial evidence was the curious conduct of the media in the Hart affair, including the *Miami Herald, Washington Post* and *Newsweek*. We received letters from Ben Bradlee at the *Post*, Tom Fiedler at the *Herald*, as well as *Playboy* magazine (which had commissioned an investigation headed by Sally Denton which they eventually abandoned), as well as Senator Hart himself.

Other than depriving the nation of the Presidency that might have been, perhaps the most nefarious aspect of the set-up was the gangland style execution of Don Aronow. Aronow was the manufacturer of the cigarette speed boats that were popular with both drug smugglers (who sometimes paid for the boats with suitcases full of cash) and, because of Aronow's friendship with George Bush and Donnie Soffer, employer of "party girl" Donna Rice and, likely, Rice herself.

Because of its popularity with drug smugglers the DEA had put Aronow's facility under surveillance, a surveillance that was inexplicably pulled a mere three hours before his gangland style murder. Although they had been close friends Bush did not attend Aronow's funeral and refused to acknowledge his widow in public, leading her to conclude that "George Bush is feeling guilty about something." Unknown to anyone outside of the government Aronow was about to be called before a Grand Jury three months prior to the execution of the set-up.

Hart was likely the target of the intelligence community for years. An unbeliever in the Warren Commission's conclusion that Lee Harvey Oswald acted alone, Hart was also instrumental in the Church Committee, that exposed CIA abuses. In 1983, Hart and Senator William Cohen, conducted a fact finding trip to Central America. His planned first stop was intended to be the VIP lounge at Managua airport. While still in the air Managua air traffic control turned back Hart's plane and it landed in Honduras. When the Senators arrived in Managua the following day, it became clear why the Sandinista air traffic controllers had warned the plane away.

The VIP lounge, at which the Senators had planned to conduct a press conference had been demolished in a Contra bombing that occurred just an hour before schedule. For the first time in the four year history of the war, the Contras had attacked the heart of Managua by air. Both the Contra pilot and co-pilot were killed in the attack and a subsequent search of the crashed airplane clearly suggested that they had had extensive contact with, if not specific direction from the CIA.

Later on that same trip the Senators also had a close call when, while flying over El Salvador the following day, there was a sudden loss of hydraulic pressure that came close to causing a crash. Upon his return to Washington then CIA director William Casey gave the Senator an audience to attempt, in the words of Bob Woodward, "to convince the Senator that no one was trying to kill him." While not all of the actors in these events might not have been aware they were being manipulated is unknown.

 Clearly in the case of the *Miami Herald* they had originally written off the "informant" as a political operative. The curious coincidence of a *Herald* reporter being on the same Miami to Washington flight with Donna Rice, and his "recognition" of her based on an inexact description raised red flags. Even more puzzling was the conduct of the *Washington Post*, which denied that they had essentially blackmailed Hart into leaving the race by showing him the results of a private investigation that they never released.

Donna Rice's background was certainly mysterious at the time. She was a jet-setter, who lived the high life, including summers aboard the yacht of Iran-Contra figure Adnan Khashoggi. Yet her professed occupation as a part-time pharmaceutic representative did not seem to be sufficient to cover her expenses. It is interesting that she, and Oliver North's secretary Fawn Hall, (who should have been charged after destroying most of North's records), shared the same publicist, Crisis Management.
I could go on, but suffice it to say, vindication after 26 years feels pretty good. Thanks Atlantic

Richard Roy Blake

LETTER TO *WESTWORD* (DENVER AREA WEEKLY)

WESTWORD KNEW THAT GARY HART MIGHT HAVE BEEN SET UP IN 1992

Thanks *Westword* and *The Atlantic Monthly*. Vindication, after 26 years. In 1992,upon investigating the many curious aspects of the demise of the Gary Hart campaign in 1988, I co-wrote a book entitled *The Gary Hart Set-up*. The book is now, and has for many years been out of print, although I now plan to reissue it, to include the newly found evidence .

In its August 12-18 in its "Off Limits" column Westword wrote: "MORE MONKEYING AROUND. First JFK then the thirtieth anniversary of Marilyn Monroe's death – at the hands of the Mafia, Robert Kennedy, Tony Curtis, a future *People* writer, take your pick. Now just when you thought it was safe to come in from the cold, up pops another conspiracy theory, this one alleging that the Gary Hart/Donna Rice imbroglio was designed to keep Hart out of the White House….(the authors) claim Hart's campaign ended as the result of a well-executed political "dirty trick" backing their theory with a string of coincidences stretching back to, yes, John F. Kennedy….Also thrown into this fine kettle of fish are a Donna Rice double, Neil and George Bush, Don Bolles, Fawn Hall and assorted CIA backed drug dealers and *Westword* (which declined to publish Blake's story)….But the really titillating media speculation concerns the late Janet Chusmir, the *Boulder Camera* publisher who moved to a far more impressive job at Knight-Ridder's *Miami Herald* and may have died 'under mysterious circumstances' because of what she knew about the Hart affair…..Paging Oliver Stone."

Jeb Bush, Ben Kramer (Meyer Lansky's nephew), Senator William Cohen, the Contras, Eden Pastora, the many witnesses with knowledge involving the Kennedy assassination (Hart did not believe the conclusions of the Warren Commission Report), and many others also comprised the rest of "kettle of fish."

At the time *Westword* turned the article down, Patricia Calhoun told me that she was not fond of conspiracy theories. Indeed in the 1990s the idea that Hart had been set up was an unconfirmed conspiracy theory. It would not be until this year that the circumstantial evidence would be corroborated by the deathbed confession of Lee Atwater.

Unfortunately *The Atlantic Monthly* article did not detail the many suspicious circumstances that suggested the set-up, including the gangland style murder of the man who knew both George Bush and Donna Rice, Don Aronow. Aronow was the manufacturer of the cigarette speed boats that were popular with both drug smugglers (who sometimes paid for the boats with suitcases full of cash) and, because of Aronow's friendship with George Bush, the DEA.

In fact, the DEA put Aronow's facility under surveillance, a surveillance that was inexplicably pulled a mere three hours before his gangland style murder. Although they had been close friends Bush did not attend Aronow's funeral and refused to acknowledge his widow in public, leading her friends to conclude that "George Bush is feeling guilty about something."

Unknown to anyone outside of the government Aronow was about to be called before a Grand Jury three months prior to the execution of the set-up.

Thanks again,

Richard Roy Blake

COVER STORY
"A NEW BOOK ASKS: WAS GARY HART SET UP?"
By R. Roy Blake

Editor: Today there is growing acceptance of political conspiracy theories, spurred by books and movies such as Oliver Stone's *JFK*. One theory currently emerging is that of authors R. Roy Blake and George R. Walters, who believe that former Colorado presidential contender and U.S. Sen. Gary Hart;s career ending brush with marital infidelity may have been orchestrated by Hart's enemies. If true, the conspiracy weaves a web that ensnares not only Hart and one time companion Donna Rice, but gangland figures, the Bush Administration and controversial Attorney General Janet Reno. Whatever is eventually proved the story offers tantalizing food for thought.

The one and only time that the State of Colorado was home to a serious presidential contender was during the 1984 and 1988 campaigns when a young

Senator who was frequently compared to John F. Kennedy threw his cowboy hat into the ring.

Conventional wisdom held that only an experienced insider with a lifetime of favors to call or an individual of great wealth had any chance of surviving in the arena. Gary Hart looked to be proving them all wrong. Hunter Thompson said it best: Hart was the closest thing we had had to a President-in-waiting in a long time.

Suddenly, over a period of five days in 1987, it was all over, thanks to Hart's well publicized affair with Donna Rice.

Three recent books suggest, however, that Hart's demise may not have been what it appeared but may have been the result of a well-orchestrated political dirty trick. The books, *Blue Thunder,* by Thomas Burdick and Charlene Mitchell, *What It Takes* by Richard Ben Cramer and *The Gary Hart Set-Up* by R. Roy Blake and George R. Walters, all credit different entities and motives for the Hart conspiracy. They do not argue about the devastating result.

In *The Gary Hart Set-Up,* we call the conspiracy a "kinder, gentler assassination" as a means of calling attention to both the political effect and the probable sponsors of the conspiracy.

Although the "smoking gun" is elusive and may have been snuffed out in a gangland style hit on Miami's "Thunderboat Alley," there are five key areas of evidence. They are:

> The strong motives attributable to both the Bush campaign and the covert operators in the CIA and elsewhere.

> The strange behavior in segments of the media, especially the *Miami Herald, Washington Post* and CBS.

> An apparent assassination attempt aimed at Hart in Nicaragua in 1983,

> The mysterious background and employments of Donna Rice.

> The apparent Bush connection to Donna Rice, Lynn Armandt, Meyer Lansky and the south Florida mob, through Miami speedboat manufacturer Don Aronow.

The last area may have resulted in the gangland style murder of Aronow a couple of months before the Hart conspiracy was complete (although the conspiracy may well have been operational for some months prior to that). There are also indications that then Dade County State Attorney and now Attorney General Janet Reno may have been a witting or unwitting accomplice in an ongoing attempt to cover up the real reasons behind the Aronow murder.

Hart was a member of the Senate Intelligence Committee and sat on the Church Committee, which aired at least some of the CIA's dirty laundry in 1975. He was a critic of the covert operations branch of the intelligence agencies and was an outspoken critic of the Warren Commission, expressing grave doubt that Lee Harvey Oswald acted alone in assassination John F. Kennedy. Perhaps more importantly, at the time, he was a vigorous opponent of the Contra war in Nicaragua and, at the time that the *Herald* broke the Hart/Rice story, Hart was leading then Vice-President Bush in a theoretical match-up by 24 points.

It was clear to the covert operators that the election of Hart would spell the end of a virtual carte blanche that they had enjoyed under the Reagan administration.

The Hart-Rice imbroglio would not have been fatal to the Hart campaign without the bizarre behavior of the media. First *Newsweek* set the tone for the Rice affair by printing unsubstantiated reports of Hart's extramarital activities.

Then the *Herald* received the famous anonymous tip that would lead to the investigation and the townhouse stakeout.

The *Herald's* first reports listed reporter Jim McGee as the recipient of the anonymous tip, but the later, more comprehensive chronology published by the *Miami Herald* listed political editor Tom Fiedler. Curiously in their letter to us, the *Herald* called the chronology "the record we wish to stand on," a statement more appropriate to a position paper than to an article.

There was more than sufficient reason to suspect that the tipster as a "dirty trickster" employed by another candidate's campaign, but rather than addressing that possibility, the *Herald* proceeded to accuse, try and convict Hart with evidence that even the newspaper later admitted was flawed. "The obvious answer is that I am being set-up," Hart responded matter-of-factly when confronted by the *Herald's* reporters.

The *Herald's* surveillance and the attendant nationwide publicity crippled but did not destroy the Hart campaign. Rice's revelations of the trip aboard the book "Monkey Business," made during a press conference on the following day, caused further damage but again were not fatal.

A bizarre twist to the affair was the supposed matter of a videotape, supposedly shot by tourists and given to CBS news, that apparently showed Hart and a blonde other than Donna Rice on board the "Monkey Business." On the same tape the tourists had filmed the same young lady strutting around in a Miami bar in a bikini in a "hot bod" contest.

The questions presented by the videotape were never examined by the press and the author's request of CBS to provide the tape for examination was ignored.

The coup-de-grace, however, was supplied in a most mysterious manner by the *Washington Post*. According to Hart aide Kevin Sweeney, the senator's first decision to abandon the campaign came after a conversation between Sweeney and a *Post* reporter, during which the reporter revealed the existence of a private detective's report in the newspaper's possession. Curiously the detective's report had been commissioned six months earlier and contents of the report were never made public. It was clear to Sweeney as well as to Hart that if Hart withdrew from the campaign the contents of the report would not be made public, although they would be revealed if he remained in the race.

If true, it was a curious role for a newspaper to play. In fact, Hart did withdraw from the race and the report was never made public.

When Hart re-entered the race such a badly damaged candidate that he was never again credible, the *Post* continued to sit on the report. Apparently either the *Post* did not really have a substantive story or the decision on whether or not to run the story was dependent on the polls. At the time the first story broke, just prior to the Iowa caucuses, Hart led all Democrats by 30 points and was 20 points ahead of George Bush.

ASSASSINATION ATTEMPTS?

On a fact finding trip to Nicaragua with Senator Cohen (also a member of the Senate Intelligence

Committee) in 1983, Hart's plane was turned back by Managua Air Traffic Control barely an hour out of the Nicaraguan capitol. The plane instead landed in Honduras.

The next day, when Cohen and Hart finally arrived in Managua, it became clear why the Sandinista air traffic controllers had warned the plane away. For the first time in the four year history of the war, the Contras had attacked the heart of Managua by air. Two 500 pound bombs had slammed into the VIP lounge where the Senators had scheduled a press conference.

The Sandinistas had apparently been prepared for the attack, as evidenced by the withering anti-aircraft barrage that knocked one of the two Contra planes out of the sky.

Documents on board the downed aircraft left little doubt that the pilots had had extensive contact with – and probably took direction from the CIA.

The near miss made Hart an extremely angry man. The CIA chief of station in Managua sought to assure him that the attack had been a rogue operation, traceable to southern front Contra leader (and important Contra cocaine figure) Eden Pastora, and that the timing was just coincidental.

The Senators could hardly have been reassured however when, while flying in a helicopter over El Salvador the following day, there was a sudden loss of hydraulic pressure, causing a 1000 foot drop in altitude and a near crash.

When a shaken Hart returned to Washington, then CIA director William Casey gave the maverick senator the one and only audience of the two men's political lives. The purpose of the meeting was, in the words of *Washington Post* reporter Bob Woodward, to attempt to convince Hart "that no one was trying to kill him."

The attack on the Managua airport was covered on the front page of the *New York Times* and virtually nowhere else. The near miss involving the two senators was completely downplayed, a fact that remains an annoyance to Hart to this day.

If one believes that the events during the senator's fact finding trip to Nicaragua were more than a coincidence, the question becomes one of motive. Three possibilities come quickly to mind. The first is that the CIA attempted to have Hart killed or badly wounded in a "plausibly deniable" fashion, perhaps to extract revenge for the Church Committee revelations. (Cohen would either be collateral damage or a secondary target, as he also sat on the Senate Intelligence Committee). The agency might also have wanted to send a message to Contra war opponents or even to nip Hart's budding political ambitions in the bud.

A second possibility is that the episodes were not a serious attempt to harm Hart, but rather a less than subtle CIA warning.

The third is that the episodes were a sort of harassment put in place to cause the senators to "keep their heads down," perhaps revise their itinerary and/or distract them from their fact-finding mission.

Whether any of these or a combination of these is correct, it quickly becomes clear the agency feared the idea of Intelligence Committee fact finding missions to Central America in 1983.

The jet set trail of Donna Rice also crosses that of the Iran Contra scandal prior to her involvement with Hart. A *Miami Herald* profile of Rice (which was amazingly available to newspapers all over the country the very moment that Rice was supposedly

identified as the woman in the *Herald's*
surveillance) stated that Rice had spent summers on
the yacht of Saudi arms merchant, Iran Contra
figure and billionaire Adnan Khashoggi.

She has hardly cashed in on her fame and is
reportedly living with a family in northern Virginia.
Offers and requests for public comment are
screened for her by the same publicist employed by
Fawn Hall, Oliver North's former secretary.
Her employments were supposedly as a full time
pharmaceutical saleswoman in the Miami area and
a part-time model and actress.

The maintenance man at her apartment complex
told the press, however, that she was rarely at
home, almost always jet setting off somewhere and
almost completely ignoring her assigned sales
territory.

One of Rice's "part time" employments was
working for Turnberry Isle Resorts and its owner
Donnie Soffer, who also owned the "Monkey
Business," was a partner of a close friend of
George Bush named Don Aronow.

Lynn Armandt, the other woman on the board the
"Monkey Business" on its infamous trip to Bimini,

also worked for Soffer. Armandt's husband was allegedly a drug dealer, who police say worked with Ben Kramer, a nephew of south Florida mob boss, Meyer Lansky.

The DEA called Kramer one of the largest drug dealers in the United States. When they raided Kramer's house, among the more unusual finds were some of the original stump speeches of Hart. Kramer was also tied to Aronow via a variety of secret deals that only surfaced when Aronow was gunned down gangland-style in February of 1987. Then Vice President George Bush had interceded with the Customs Service , which awarded Aronow, a speedboat manufacturer, the contract to build drug interdiction boats. The DEA, however, suspected Aronow of selling the same sorts of speedboats to smugglers for cash, with no questions asked. As a result they put Aronow's factory under surveillance.

It was later revealed that Aronow was to be scheduled to be subpoenaed before a federal grand jury. Some suspected that he was murdered because it was thought he might talk.
The information about who will be subpoenaed before a grand jury is supposedly secret and is

certainly only available to those in the federal government.

One of the things Aronow might have been able to talk about was the connection among George Bush, Donna Rice and/or Ben Kramer.

If then Dade county prosecutor and now Attorney General Janet Reno has her way, however, Kramer will not be talking to anyone soon. Instead he will be on Florida's death row, convicted of the Aronow murder.

In the aftermath of the Aronow murder it became obvious to investigative reporters that witnesses were being intimidated and that the investigation was being deliberately misled.Reno and the rest of the Dade County power structure used a jailhouse snitch to accuse another inmate – who matched none of the eyewitness descriptions in the murder – to try and wrap up the loose ends.

At first the snitch turned out to be a bit of a loose cannon. The original reason for the killing was a drug deal gone sour, allegedly involving Jeb Bush, George's son and now a candidate for the governor's office in Florida, as being one of the principals. After eliminating the Bush name from

141

the accusations, the authorities proceeded to indict Robert "Bobby" Young and Ben Kramer for the murder, despite the fact that the snitch had nearly every verifiable detail about the crime wrong.

LOOSE ENDS

Playboy magazine, which had commissioned its own investigative team to investigate the Hart affair, decided to spike the story after almost a year of research. According to Senior Editor Peter Moore, *Playboy* decided it could not trust their sources.

One of those sources, according to Sally Denton, author of the *Bluegrass Conspiracy* and one of the authors commissioned by *Playboy* claimed to be "the fed who did the job" on Hart.

A widely held view, heard frequently on talk radio shows, is that Hart got what was coming to him and that even if Rice had been deliberately set in Hart's path, the fact that Hart fell for what is commonly referred to as a "honey pot" agent is one's fault but Hart's.

Perhaps most frustrating of all is Hart's steadfast

refusal to give out an interview on the events that led to his decision to abandon politics.

Hart also was not helpful in our investigation, sending us a letter stating that he was refusing to give us permission to request his Freedom of Information Act files with the CIA, State Department, etc., "for the very simple reason that I (Hart) do not know what those files contain." His final words to us, like Hart himself, were enigmatic: "I will not comment on the circumstances which caused me to decide to withdraw from politics. The facts and circumstances must speak for themselves. Eventually the correct interpretation will emerge."

EDITORS NOTE:

About the author...

R. Roy Blake is an investigative journalist who has written freelance articles for the *Colorado Springs Sun*, *Rocky Mountain News*, *Colorado Daily* and other publications.

Apart from *The Gary Hart Set-Up,* he is currently working on a book entitled, Propaganda Assets, which examines the media's role in wittingly and refusal to give out an interview on the events that led to his decision to abandon politics.

Hart also was not helpful in our investigation, sending us a letter stating that he was refusing to give us permission to request his Freedom of Information Act files with the CIA, State Department, etc., "for the very simple reason that I (Hart) do not know what those files contain." His final words to us, like Hart himself, were enigmatic: "I will not comment on the circumstances which caused me to decide to withdraw from politics. The facts and circumstances must speak for themselves. Eventually the correct interpretation will emerge."

EDITORS NOTE:

About the author…

R. Roy Blake is an investigative journalist who has written freelance articles for the *Colorado Springs Sun*, *Rocky Mountain News*, *Colorado Daily* and other publications.

Apart from *The Gary Hart Set-Up,* he is currently working on a book entitled, Propaganda Assets, which examines the media's role in wittingly and unwittingly distributing governmentally inspired and other disinformation to the public.

The Gary Hart Set-Up, published by Laramide Productions, Inc. in Aurora, is soon to be listed in Books in Print and will be available for commercial distribution next fall.

BIBLIOGRAPHY

Bai, Matt, *All the Truth is Out, The Week Politics Went Tabloid.* New York: Alfred A. Knopf, 2014.

Blake, R. Roy, *Objective Evil: Satanic Cults in US Intelligence.* Aurora, Colorado: Laramide Productions, 1995.

Blake, R. Roy and George R. Walters, *The Gary Hart Set-Up*, Aurora, Colorado: Laramide Productions, 1992.

Blakey, G. Robert and Richard N. Billings, *The Plot to Kill the President.* New York: Times Books, 1981.

Burdick, Thomas and Charlene Mitchell, *Blue Thunder.* New York: Simon and Schuster, 1990.

Eddy, Paul with Hugh Sabogal and Sara Walden, *The Cocaine Wars.* New York-London: W.W. Norton, Co., 1988.

Fallows, James, "Was Gary Hart Set Up?" *Atlantic* 2018

Hougan, Jim, *Spooks, The Haunting of America – The Private Use of Secret Agents.* New York: William Morrow and Co., 1978.

McCoy, Alfred, *The Politics of Heroin in Southeast Asia.* New York: Harper and Row, 1972.

Ranelaugh, John, *The Agency, the Rise and Decline of the CIA.* New York: Simon and Schuster

Smith, Joseph Burkholder, *Portrait of a Cold Warrior.* New York: G.P. Putnam's Sons, 1976.

Subcommittee on Terrorism, Narcotics and International Operations of the Committee on Foreign Relations of the United States Senate, *Drugs, Law Enforcement and Foreign Policy,* Washington, D.C.: U.S. Government Printing Office 96-845, 1989.

The Denver Post, Denver News Media, Inc.

Unger, Craig, "October Surprise," *Esquire* magazine (October 1991): 92-181.

Woodward, Robert, *Veil: The Secret Wars of the CIA 1981-1987.* New York: Simon and Schuster, 1987.

LINKS

The November 2018 *Atlantic* article "Was Gary Hart Set Up?" by James Fallows

https://www.theatlantic.com/magazine/archive/2018/11/was-gary-hart-set-up/570802/

***Miami Herald* article reporting the *New York Times* "outing" of the Hart affair tipster**

https://www.miamiherald.com/news/local/article2185644.html

"Genetic Bullets" article on Rense.com

https://rense.com/general18/spbio.htm

"Genetic Bullets" article on Washington Free Press website

http://wafreepress.org/43/genetic.html

Project Censored awards 2001 #16
"Human Genome Project Opens the Door to Ethnically Specific Biological Weapons"

https://www.projectcensored.org/16-human-genome-project-opens-the-door-to-ethnically-specific-bioweapons/

Ex-CIA agent Chip Tatum Youtube video mentioning Gary Hart set up

https://www.youtube.com/watch?v=lyYnFTIY-3M

Local Miami Article on Aronow Murder Case

WWW.MIAMIBEACH411.COM/NEWS/DON-
ARONOW

Made in the USA
San Bernardino, CA
11 December 2018